New Perspectives in associatic

THE FISHERMEN
BY CHIGOZIE OBIOMA

ADAPTED FOR THE STAGE BY
GBOLAHAN OBISESAN

The Fishermen was first performed on 19 July 2018
at HOME in Manchester

New Perspectives is supported using public funding
by Arts Council England.
Registered Charity No: 1053809

NEW PERSPECTIVES

New Perspectives is an East Midlands-based touring theatre company, specialising in bringing new work to rural and community audiences. Through an annual programme of original adaptations, rare revivals and new writing, we aim to bring live theatre that is vital, affordable and accessible into the heart of wide-ranging communities, as well as to regional, national and international venues.

Our work tours nationally and internationally, from small rural village halls to 700-seat theatres. Our mixed economy touring models enable us to tour and programme live performances in the heart of communities, affording opportunities for those with little or no access to other cultural outlets the opportunities to see high quality performances right on their doorstep. Removing barriers of location, age, culture or socio-economic status fuels our ambition to bring audiences into close contact with the highest quality new work.

- Creating a diverse brand of live theatre that is nationally and internationally recognised as challenging, original and unafraid to take bold creative risks

- Empowering artists and theatre makers across the region with knowledge, skills and increasing networks through the development of small-scale and rural touring theatre

- Engaging regional audiences by widening access to high quality live performance regardless of age, social class, ethnicity, gender, disability or geographic location

We maintain the highest levels of artistry and production values in all our work, and deliver a programme of wide cultural significance and are therefore able to advance the arts through regular critical analysis of the work we create. Our productions are testament to the fact that rural theatre is as relevant, challenging and dynamic as theatre made for any other environment.

Artistic Director Jack McNamara
Executive Director Sally Anne Tye

To find out more:

www.newperspectives.co.uk

twitter: twitter.com/NPtheatre
facebook: facebook.com/newperspectivestheatrecompany
youtube: youtube.com/user/newperspectivesTV
flickr: flickr.com/photos/npimagegallery/

THE FISHERMEN BY CHIGOZIE OBIOMA
ADAPTED FOR THE STAGE BY GBOLAHAN OBISESAN

Cast (in alphabetical order)

MICHAEL AJAO	Ben
VALENTINE OLUKOGA	Obembe

Creative & Production Team

JACK McNAMARA	Director
ANGHARAD JONES	Associate Director
AMELIA JANE HANKIN	Designer
AMY MAE	Lighting Designer
POETICAL MACHINES	Sound Designer
KITTY WINTER	Movement
ALI BAKEWELL/ ORAN O'NEILL	Stage Manager
ALISON WILLCOX	Production Manager
VICKY RICHARDSON CDG	Casting

New Perspectives

JACK McNAMARA	Artistic Director
SALLY ANNE TYE	Executive Director
ALISON WILLCOX	Production Manager
KARA COLE	Communications and Administrative Assistant
JAYNE WILLIAMS	Participation Director
NEALE BIRCH	Producer
ZOE KEEN	Bookkeeper

Filming by Charlotte Seegers
Special thanks to Petra Tauscher and the fantastic team at HOME, Frances Connor, Robert Day, Ruth Disney, Pamela Raith and Charlotte Seegers.

New Perspectives is supported using funding by Arts Council England

As a registered charity No. 1053809 to find out how you might help to make a difference see www.newperspectives.co.uk or contact Sally@newperspectives.co.uk

Cast and Creative Team

© Robert Day

Michael Ajao | Ben

Michael recently appeared in *Br'er Cotton* at Theatre503.

'Michael Ajao is superb as the hot-headed, soft-hearted teenage revolutionary, his swagger suggesting an air of adopted certainty...' Matt Trueman, *WhatsOnStage*

He previously appeared in *The Lorax* at the Old Vic.

He made his screen debut in *Attack the Block* directed by Joe Cornish, and also played the role of Corey Draper in Tiger Aspect's *Cuffs* for BBC. He was recently on tour with the Regent's Park Open Air Theatre's production of *Lord of the Flies* as Maurice, following his appearance in *Liberian Girl* at the Royal Court.

Michael attended the BRIT School.

© Robert Day

Valentine Olukoga | Obembe

Valentine began as a prospect with Synergy Theatre Project. Since his 2012 stage debut in *Glengarry Glen Ross* at HMP Brixton he has appeared in many theatre productions including *Cape* (Synergy Theatre Project/ Unicorn Theatre) and *The Suicide* (National Theatre). He is most recognised for his roles as Killer in the Royal Court's *Liberian Girl*, and as Brandon in ITV's *Unforgotten*.

© Zach Mueller

Chigozie Obioma | Writer

Chigozie Obioma was born in Akure, Nigeria. His debut novel, *The Fishermen*, is winner of the inaugural FT/Oppenheimer Award for Fiction, the NAACP Image Awards for Debut Literary Work, and the Art Seidenbaum Award for First Fiction (Los Angeles Times Book Prizes), and was a finalist for the Man Booker Prize 2015, as well as for several other prizes in the US and UK. Obioma was named one of Foreign Policy's 100 Leading Global Thinkers of 2015. *The Fishermen* has been translated into 25 languages and adapted into a stage play. He is an assistant professor of Literature and Creative Writing at the University of Nebraska-Lincoln.

Gbolahan Obisesan | Stage Adapter

Gbolahan Obisesan was the Genesis Fellow of the Young Vic Theatre. He is currently developing a feature film with Emu Films/Film 4.

Theatre includes: *Yvette* (China Plate); *Feast* (Royal Court/Young Vic); *Cuttin it* (Olivier nominated; Young Vic, Sheffield Crucible, Birmingham Rep, Yard Theatre, Royal Court); *How Nigeria Became: A story, and a spear that didn't work* (Unicorn Theatre); *We Are Proud to Present...* (Bush Theatre); *Pigeon English* (Bristol Old Vic/Edinburgh Festival); *Mad About The Boy* (Edinburgh Festival and UK tour). Upcoming work includes: *Hansel and Gretel* (The Place/Uchenna Dance).

Directing credits include: *66 books* (Bush Theatre); *SUS* (Young Vic and UK tour; Jerwood Award for directing); *Eye/Balls* and *Hold it Up*(Soho Theatre). He was Director in Residence at the National Theatre Studio, and resident director for *Fela!* (National Theatre). Upcoming directing includes: *random* (Leeds Playhouse).

Jack McNamara | Director

Jack has been Artistic Director of New Perspectives since September 2012. Productions for the company include: *The Boss of It All* by Lars von Trier (Assembly Roxy, Edinburgh, and Soho Theatre); *The Lovesong of Alfred J Hitchcock* by David Rudkin (Brits Off-Broadway, New York and UK tour); *Him With His Foot In His Mouth* by Saul Bellow and *Watching the Living* by Jane Upton, adapted from two Daphne du Maurier short stories (both UK tours); *HOOD* (150th Anniversary Commission, Nottingham Theatre Royal); *Darkness Darkness* (Nottingham Playhouse co-production); *Harvest* (regional tour) and *Sisyphus* (BE Festival, Mess Award winner).

Plays for children and family audiences include: *The Tiger's Bones and Other* Stories (UK tour) and most recently *The Giant Jam Sandwich* (UK tour and Edinburgh).

Previous productions as director include: *Exterminating Angel* (Basement Brighton/Pleasance Edinburgh/UK tour); *Texts for Nothing* by Samuel Beckett (The Rest is Noise Festival, Southbank Centre); *The Word for Snow* by Don DeLillo (London Literature Festival, Southbank Centre); *Malaise Trio* (Camden People's Theatre); *Instructions for John Howell* by Julio Cortazar (Nursery Festival); *Betrayal* by Harold Pinter (Nuffield, Southampton); *The Blind* by Maurice Maeterlinck (Arcola Theatre); *Lucid Dreams for Higher Living* (Underbelly, Edinburgh); *Valparaiso* by Don DeLillo (Old Red Lion); *A Cool Million* by Nathanael West (Underbelly, Edinburgh); *Little Malcolm and His Struggle Against the Eunuchs* (Warwick Arts Centre).

Previously, Jack was Assistant Director at the Royal Shakespeare Company and director on attachment at the Nuffield Theatre Southampton under the Regional Theatre Young Director Scheme. Independently, Jack continues to make experimental theatre through his company Future Ruins, and will direct *Love Lies Bleeding* by Don DeLillo at the Printroom in November 2018.

Angharad Jones | Associate Director

Angharad Jones is co-founder and Joint Artistic Director of Fifth Word.

Directing credits for Fifth Word include: *Lava* by James Fritz (world premiere, Nottingham Playhouse); *Bones* by Jane Upton (Edinburgh Fringe Festival, Tristan Bates and UK tour); *Painkillers* by Paul Buie (Edinburgh Fringe Festival, East Midlands tour).

Angharad was associate director on *All The Little Lights* by Jane Upton (Nottingham Playhouse, UK Tour, Arcola Theatre 2017; Nominated for Off West End Award for Best New Play and Joint Winner of the George Devine Award).

Amelia Jane Hankin | Designer

Amelia trained at RADA and the RSC.

Upcoming design credits include: *The Comedy of Errors* (RSC); *Gastronomic* (Curious Directive).

Recent design credits include: *Mountains: The Dreams of Lily Kwok* (Royal Exchange Studio Theatre/national tour); *Smack That (a conversation)* (Barbican); *Confidence* (Southwark Playhouse); *Europe After the Rain* (Mercury Theatre); *Mixed Brain* (Tiata Fahodzi and Paines Plough); *The Scar Test* (Soho Theatre); *Punts* (Theatre503); *Natives* (Southwark Playhouse); *PowerPlay* (Historic Royal Palaces); *Good Dog* (Watford Palace Theatre); *The Same Deep Water As Me* (Guildhall); *Rudolf* (West Yorkshire Playhouse); *The Crucible* (Guildhall); *Torch* (Edinburgh Festival); *We Are You* (Young Vic); *Bricks and Pieces* (RADA/Latitude); *The Neighbourhood Project* (Bush Theatre); *This is Art* (Shakespeare in Shoreditch); *The Tiger's Bones* (Polka and West Yorkshire Playhouse); *The Little Prince* (Arcola Theatre); *Pinter Triple Bill and Dealer's Choice* (Guildhall); *Night Before Christmas* (West Yorkshire Playhouse); *She Called Me Mother* (Tara Arts and national tour); *Fake It 'Til You Make It* with Bryony Kimmings and Tim Grayburn (national tour, Traverse Theatre, and Soho Theatre); and *64 Squares* with Rhum and Clay (national tour and Edinburgh Festival).

Amy Mae | Lighting Designer

Amy works across theatre, dance, site specific and devised performance.

Amy designed the lighting for the acclaimed 'Pie Shop' version of *Sweeny Todd: The Demon Barber of Fleet Street*, which is currently playing at the Barrow Street Theatre in New York. She won the Knight of Illumination Award in 2015 for the London production, and her designs for the New York production have been nominated for the 2017 Drama Desk Award for Outstanding Lighting Design and the Lucille Lortel Award for Best Lighting.

Recent Credits include: *Br'er Cotton* (Theatre503); *Mountains: The Dreams of lily Kwok* (Royal Exchange); *Exploding Circus* (Pavilion Theatre, Worthing); *Othello, Jeckyll and Hyde* and *The Host* (NYT Rep Season 2017); *Half Breed* (Talawa, Soho Theatre & Assembly Rooms); *Start*

Swimming (Young Vic/Summerhall Edinburgh); *The Ugly One* (Park Theatre); *Babette's Feast* (The Print Room); *The Lounge* (Soho Theatre); *Wordswroth* (Theatre By the Lake); *Paradise of Assassins* (Tara Theatre); *Knife Edge* (Pond Restaurant, Dalston); *Miniaturists 55* (Arcola Theatre); *Prize Fights* (Royal Academy of Dramatic Art); *Orphans* (Southwark Playhouse); *Macbeth* (Italia Conti); *I'm Not Here Right Now* (Paines Plough's Roundabout and Soho Theatre); *Liolà* (New Diorama Theatre); *Children in Uniform*, *Punk Rock* (Tristan Bates Theatre); *Sweeney Todd* (Harringtons Pie and Mash Shop and West End); *The Tree Sisters* (Cockpit Theatre); *Cat Couture* (Music Video); *In Bed* (London Theatre Workshop); *Henry V* (Royal Academy of Dramatic Art); *Pool*, *The Gut Girls* (Brockley Jack Theatre); *The Legacy* (The Place).

Programming credits Include: *Jeux* (Royal Opera House); *Tannhauser* (Longborough Festival Opera); *Robin Hood* (Theatre Royal Stratford East); *Lela & Co.* (Royal Court); *dirty butterfly* and *Red Forest* (The Young Vic).

She was one of the invited speakers at the 2017 Showlight Conference in Florence. Amy trained at RADA on the postgraduate Stage Electrics and Lighting Design course and has a degree in Stage Management and Performing Arts from the University of Winchester. www.amymaelighting.com

Adam McCready for Poetical Machines LTD |
Composer/ Sound Designer

Poetical Machines create bespoke music and audio projects for live theatre and dance productions, museums, galleries, film, radio and podcasts, in addition to developing drama projects based on science and technology themes.

Credits include: *Brighton Rock* (Pilot Theatre/York Theatre Royal UK tour); *The Beautiful Game* (Next Door Dance); *Two* (Derby Theatre); *Jump Out of Skin* (Pleasance Theatre, London/GLYPT); *Interlude* (Maison Foo); *World Cultures Gallery Interactive Soundscape Installation*, *Finding Lines Exhibition* (Derby Museums); *Call of the Wild* (Greenwich Theatre/GLYPT); *Sweeney Todd* (Derby Theatre and Mercury Theatre); *Getting Better Slowly* (Adam Pownall UK tour); *Holes*, *Town Mouse and Country Mouse*, *The Cherry Orchard*, *The Princess and the Frog*, *Aladdin*, *The Glass Menagerie*, *Any Means Necessary*, *Hare and Tortoise*, *A Skull in Connemara*, *Arcadia*, *How to Breathe* (Nottingham Playhouse); *What the Butler Saw*, *A Streetcar Named Desire*, *Shiv* (Curve, Leicester); *Oh Whistle and I'll Come...*, *Playland*, *Haunts*, *He Wore a Red Hat*, *Watching the Living*, *Wasteland*, *Honeyman* (New Perspectives); *Snow Queen* (Little Pixie Productions); *Private Lives*, *Noises Off*, *Educating Rita*, *Saturday Night and Sunday Morning*, *Arsenic and Old Lace*, *Betty Blue Eyes*, *The Butterfly Lion* (Mercury Theatre); *The Mountaintop*, *The Dumb Waiter*, *A Kind of Alaska*, *The Merchant of Venice* (Derby Live); *Love Already* (Ovalhouse); *Tongues* (Tristan Bates Theatre); *Edward II* (BAC); *Down the Line* (Barrow Hill Roundhouse).

Currently in development for 2019: *ADA, The Life and Legacy of Ada Lovelace*.

Website: poeticalmachines.co.uk Twitter: @PoeticalMachine

Kitty Winter | Movement

Kitty is a movement director, choreographer and director, based in Derbyshire and London, UK. She trained in contemporary dance and choreography at Trinity Laban, and on the acclaimed movement MA at the Royal Central School of Speech and Drama.

Recent movement credits include: *The Kite Runner* (Nottingham Playhouse/UK Productions, Playhouse Theatre and Wyndham's Theatre London/UK tour); *Here I Belong, Wolves are Coming for You, As the Crow Flies* (Pentabus Theatre); *Peter Pan, Alice in Wonderland, Cinderella, A Christmas Carol, The Rise and Fall of Little Voice* (Derby Theatre); *Harvest* (New Perspectives); *Blood* (Tamasha/Belgrade Theatre Coventry); *Rapunzel, Jack* and *Tom's Midnight Garden* (Nottingham Playhouse); *Tiny Treasures, The Night Pirates* (Theatre Hullabaloo); *The Dog House, Puss in Boots, Women on the Verge of HRT* (Derby LIVE).

Recent directing credits include: *Spinning Yarns, FIVE* (Theatre Hullabaloo/Theatre Direct, Canada); *Car Story* (Box Clever Theatre); *Whose Shoes?* (Nottingham Playhouse); *Awaking Durga* (Kali Theatre/ Soho Theatre).

Kitty is Co-Artistic Director of WinterWalker. For the company she has recently directed and produced *The Nutcracker and the Mouse King* (Watermans Arts Centre/Déda/Lincoln Drill Hall) and *Three Keepers* (UK tour).

Director's Note

Chigozie Obioma was just twenty-nine when his debut novel about brothers torn apart by a prophecy was published in 2015. The book was a global success, announcing him as a major new voice on the international literary scene. As soon as I read it I saw glimpses of a play. Yet given what hot property the book was, I never expected its celebrated young author to be so receptive and generous to a touring theatre company on the other side of the world wanting to turn it into a stage play.

From the beginning, the vision for the play differed considerably from the book. Whilst the novel is a family saga populated by many characters, the play boils the action down to just two people. We still meet the other characters, but only through the prism of two brothers who have lived through the story. I am fascinated with the idea that siblings hold traces of their wider family within them. An encounter between siblings can become a confrontation with one's parents or other siblings; a notion that gives this play its particular dramatic engine.

Gbolahan Obisesan has dived into the novel and found the play its own voice. Gbolahan grew up in Nigeria until the age of ten, which is also the age of the book's protagonist. He knows this world intimately and has captured its language in all its idiosyncrasy.

Our rehearsal room has been a place of complete collaboration, with two actors, Michael Ajao and Valentine Olukoga, building the show with myself and Associate Director, Angharad Jones, from the ground up.

We hope our distilled stage version captures the true spirit of the book and draws out its dramatic core. The dark story of the Agwu family has been an exciting place to live and we are delighted to be able to bring it to audiences, live for the first time.

Jack McNamara
Artistic Director
New Perspectives Theatre Company

THE FISHERMEN

Adapted for the stage by
Gbolahan Obisesan

From the novel by
Chigozie Obioma

'There is no story that is not true... The world has no end, and what is good among one people is an abomination with others.'

Things Fall Apart, Chinua Achebe

Characters

BEN
OBEMBE

Note on Text

Lines in italics indicate that the brothers are role-playing other characters.

Stage directions are (italicised and in brackets).

Words of dialogue in [square brackets] can either be said or omitted.

A dash (–) indicates an interruption or change in thought/intention in dialogue.

A forward slash (/) indicates an interruption by another character, or lines spoken simultaneously.

An ellipsis (…) indicates a trailing-off of thought or a delayed response.

This edition features the full-length version of the play.
A shortened version was first performed at the Edinburgh
Festival Fringe 2018.

This text went to press before the end of rehearsals and so may differ slightly from the play as performed.

1.

(*At Omi-Ala, Nigeria.*

BEN *looks across the Omi-Ala river.*

Sombre and relaxed.

OBEMBE *arrives at the riverbank and notices his brother. He walks forward and stands parallel as they both look across the water.*)

BEN. I thought we would never see each other again

OBEMBE. This is the… place I thought I would see you –

BEN. Omi-Ala –

OBEMBE. Water splits

BEN. It certainly does –

OBEMBE. I brought a gift –

BEN. A gift

OBEMBE. For our brother –

BEN. You brought a gift? –

OBEMBE. I just thought… it might… be appropriate –

BEN. Like a peace offering? –

OBEMBE. Exactly

BEN. I can't see it –

OBEMBE. It's wrapped – It's what you do with a gift

BEN. …What is it?

OBEMBE. It's rude to ask and anyway it's not for you. That's why I came here.

BEN. Of all places.

OBEMBE. Still as eerie as I remember. We were fishermen.

BEN. We were fishermen

(*They look at each other.*)

OBEMBE. We are fishermen. It's good to see you brother.

BEN. I have dreamt…

OBEMBE. What? What did you dream?

BEN.…A different meeting. I imagine you also…

OBEMBE. Had nightmares.

BEN. Of all of the things I suffered for.

OBEMBE. We all suffered.

BEN. You disappeared.

OBEMBE. I suffered too –

BEN. The fact I am alive is a miracle –

OBEMBE. But you did it –

BEN. Once you get caught for a crime – you sort of don't have a choice –

OBEMBE. Unless you run –

BEN. With a guilty conscience –

OBEMBE. And a sore neck from constantly looking over my shoulder –

BEN. If you don't do the time – you'll always be followed by…

OBEMBE. You resent me –

BEN. I don't know – I haven't made up my mind –

OBEMBE. So, you want to torment me –

BEN. if it helps –

OBEMBE. I don't see how…

BEN. Of course you don't –

OBEMBE. What's that supposed to mean?

BEN. Why are you here?

OBEMBE. I needed to come –

BEN. Why?

OBEMBE. I brought a gift –

BEN. So what –

OBEMBE. Okay, I haven't thought it through

BEN. What's the point of talking to you?

OBEMBE. What do you want to hear?

   (*Pause.*)

BEN. Could we have stopped it, changed it? (*Pause.*)
   Everything.

OBEMBE. How? – It was impossible –

BEN. You don't know that –

OBEMBE. It was prophesied

BEN. The things that happened were –

OBEMBE. / Inevitable

BEN. / Incidental –

OBEMBE. You're in denial –

BEN. I know what happened –

OBEMBE. So do I – You think you're the only one affected –
   I'm affected – so was Mother and Father – so was –

BEN. The map of dreams.

OBEMBE. Ha! Father's ascribed occupation for us.

BEN. I was going to become a professor.

OBEMBE. That's not what you wanted to be.

BEN. You were supposed to be the family doctor – Boja a
lawyer and Ikenna / a pilot

OBEMBE. a pilot. (*With relish*.) We all wanted to be the family
pilot.

BEN. Yes, but no one, not even Father knew what I wanted to be.

OBEMBE. A veterinarian.

BEN. Ah, you remembered!

OBEMBE. Only because I looked it up in the Britannica
Encyclopedia. I have the facts stored up in here – (*Taps his
head*.)

BEN. What facts do you have?

OBEMBE. I remember a lot of things I'm sure you forgot –

BEN. Try me –

OBEMBE. Okay – why did we become fishermen? –

BEN. That's easy…

OBEMBE. …So?… what's the answer?

BEN. Because we stopped playing football –

OBEMBE. But why did we stop playing football?

BEN. We weren't very good –

OBEMBE. Did we play football regularly?

BEN. Only when Father wasn't around –

OBEMBE. But why?

BEN (*as Father*). *Because academics are more valuable than
sportsmen.*

OBEMBE. It's a lie –

BEN. Argue that with Father –

OBEMBE. But when did the games stop –

BEN. Now you're speaking in riddles –

OBEMBE. because you don't remember –

BEN. Whatever it is – what you're thinking – the reason – I
    remember

OBEMBE. But you haven't said it –

BEN. I don't need to say it

OBEMBE. You are being evasive –

BEN. I can be what I want when I like –

OBEMBE. So you don't remember the letter –

BEN. there are twenty-six of them in the alphabet – which one
    specifically? –

OBEMBE. The letter Father received from Yola –

BEN. Did you read it?

OBEMBE. Of course not – it was Father's letter –

BEN. Why are we talking about this letter?

OBEMBE. You don't remember – ? (*As Mother.*) *We are not
    going to church today I have some things to do before your
    father leaves.*

BEN. Mummy doesn't sound like that – And her mannerisms
    are a bit more considered –

OBEMBE. It's how I remember her –

BEN. Well you're wrong –

OBEMBE. Why don't you show me then?

BEN (*as Mother*). *Okay… What kind of job takes a man away
    from –*

OBEMBE (*laughing*). Okay… maybe drop your hip more

BEN. It's in the voice okay – I have her voice, leave me –

OBEMBE (*stifling giggles*). well then, your portrayal is
    exceptional

BEN (*flippantly*). I know… (*As Mother.*) *What kind of job takes a man away from his family?*

OBEMBE (*as Father*). *It is the bank – Do you want them to stop employing me?*

BEN. Wow –

OBEMBE. What?

BEN. That was quite scary – You sound exactly like him –

OBEMBE. He shouted at me enough –

BEN (*giggling*). Yes that's true –

OBEMBE. Okay, okay – where were we –

BEN (*as Mother*). *But why are you being transferred? They know you have a wife and children – children I can't raise by myself.*

OBEMBE (*as Father*). *And with the transfer, comes a different pay grade and we can raise the children more securely.*

BEN (*as Mother*). *So what? They can't pay you for doing the same job here in Akure?*

OBEMBE (*as Father*). *Nigeria is a big country with expanding infrastructures – the Central Bank of Nigeria is part of that expansion*

BEN (*as Mother*). *So will your children – expand – especially while their father is away.*

OBEMBE (*as Father*). *Habba!*

BEN (*as Mother*). *Growing boys Emeka*

OBEMBE (*as Father*). *With school fees – not to mention clothes – food and rent for the roof above our heads.*

BEN (*as Mother*). *All that responsibility falls on you does it? Whether you admit to see it or not I work just as hard as you*

OBEMBE (*as Father*). *You run a fresh-food stall…*

BEN (*as Mother*). *A very reliable one – which requires a lot of due diligence in unsociable hours – on top of that – making sure the house does not burn down – literally – instilling respect and helpfulness into our children, but the rest is your portion.*

OBEMBE (*as Father*). *Okay so I'm asking you to cover me.*

BEN (*as Mother*). *I can't do that indefinitely.*

OBEMBE (*as Father*). *Now you're exaggerating – I will speak to the boys and they will deliver on my portion.*

(*They both laugh.*)

You were eight.

BEN. I was nine and you were ten, Boja was thirteen.

OBEMBE. So Ikenna was fourteen.

BEN. We were both in the room when Father came in.

OBEMBE (*as Father*). *Ikenna! Boja!*

BOTH (*as Boja and Ikenna*). *Yes sir?*

OBEMBE (*as Father*). *Obembe, Ben!*

BOTH. Yes sir?

OBEMBE (*as Father*). *Your mother and I have decided I will start living in Yola from this day onwards.*

BEN. Yola? Where is that? Is it overseas?

OBEMBE (*as Father*). *It is still here in Nigeria – In the central far east – Quite close to Cameroon*

BEN. That far? – You might possibly see Roger Milla –

OBEMBE (*as Father*). *Perhaps not out of my window but if he's in Nigeria in the district I'm staying – yes, maybe.*

BEN. If you see him, he must do his dance for you and sign a football for us.

OBEMBE (*as Father*). *Nonsense – Listen, I came in to tell you – I don't want you boys to give your mother any troubles whatsoever – I will call her regularly and if I hear any disappointing news and I mean any funny business at all – I will give you the guerdon for them – Now take this –* (*Handing them money.*)

BEN. I wanted it to be proper bribe – *big money* – but it was just our pocket money.

OBEMBE. That allowance money was small shah – considering how long Father was away – even Ikenna and Boja just got one more note each than us. It was that letter that sent Daddy away, which meant we had more freedom.

BEN (*as Mother*). *Eme – remember you have growing boys here.*

OBEMBE. What did we buy with our pocket money?

OBEMBE *holds up his bag shaped like a football.*

BEN. I wonder what it is

OBEMBE. The gift –

OBEMBE *gets the football out of his bag.*

BEN. Atlanta 1996 Olympic Games replica –

OBEMBE. It's beautiful –

BEN. Boja always prayed for the ball –

OBEMBE (*as Boja*). *Father Lord Jesus – help us keep this football for much longer and prevent the force of the kick from our legs taking it across the clearing. This football will not be the instrument or victim of destruction – it will avoid windows, crippled old men or pinballing off the head of an unsuspecting passer-by – Amen.*

BEN (*dribbling the ball*). Ikenna played skilfully – dribbling with the inventiveness of Jay-Jay Okocha.

OBEMBE. I was a goalkeeping daredevil like René Higuita.

BEN. You're now making up names.

OBEMBE. He was the Colombian Superman with the scorpion save against England in 1995.

BEN. Oh yeah, okay I remember.

OBEMBE. I was like a cat.

BEN. Obembe Higuicat.

OBEMBE. I like that – we should have called me that –

BEN. Boja was more defensive than skilful –

OBEMBE. Mainly lashing the ball as far as he could for fear of being labelled an ineffective defender by Ikenna –

BEN. I was always made the water-and-fetch boy – but I remember I couldn't collect the ball –

OBEMBE. Because Boja made a rugby clearance. (*Kicks the ball.*)

BEN. Boja look at what your oversized foot has done – Were you aiming for the sun? –

OBEMBE (*as Boja*). *What are you talking – I just scattered their attack –*

BEN. The whole game and the ball is now a casualty of your reckless scatter –

OBEMBE. the commentator would say…

BEN. That backyard is impenetrable – It belongs to the medical doctor – that ball is gone for sure

OBEMBE (*as Boja*). *We must at least try – He has to be a kind man on account of his caring profession – it is our mission to retrieve the ball and continue the game –*

BEN (*as Doctor*). *You obstinate children – you urchins of the gutter – you dare enter my compound –*

OBEMBE (*out of breath*). That was a disastrous mission to undertake –

BEN. I'm glad he didn't have dogs – an Alsatian – he looks like an Alsatian type of medical doctor – A doctor of the Gestapo –

OBEMBE. Do you think he works for white people?

BEN. When they build fences that big, for big football clearances to fly over – he is some sort of errand boy for the white government –

OBEMBE. Oyinbo government? – But why would he be living here –

BEN. It's either for espionage or / sabotage

OBEMBE. Sabotage

BEN. Espionage

OBEMBE. They both said sabotage together –

BEN. Ikenna definitely said espionage –

OBEMBE. You would say that –

BEN. That is how I remember it –

OBEMBE. Okay, so then we became fishermen.

2.

BEN. It was at the end of January

OBEMBE. January 18th 1996

BEN. Correct… how did you – ?

OBEMBE. ah ah, that one's easy now – Boja's fourteenth birthday –

BEN. had been celebrated that weekend –

OBEMBE. For one month, Boja would be the same age as Ikenna until Ikenna turned fifteen

BEN. On the 10th February –

OBEMBE. Then they were no longer age-mates and Ikenna was the eldest again

BEN. Ikenna bought the hooked fishing lines

OBEMBE. After his friend Solomon said

BEN (as Solomon). *o boy it's a thrilling experience o – My guy, you go catch fish and sell for market / it's all I need*

OBEMBE (singing). 'It's alllllllllll I neeeeeeeed to get byyyyyy i i – Fishing is allllllllllllll I neeeeeeeed to get byy i i'

BEN. Mary J. Blige is a much better singer than you will ever be –

OBEMBE. Well I didn't sing it like Mary Blige – I sang it like Solomon –

BEN. J. – Mary – Mary. J. Blige – J. Blige –

OBEMBE. You are done… Ikenna really wanted to fish, so we maybe could have another Yoyodon for our empty fish bowl –

BEN. Symphysodon –

OBEMBE. it was a discus fish –

BEN. of the Symphysodon species –

OBEMBE. I named it Yoyodon – Father agreed –

BEN. because you couldn't pronounce Symphysodon –

OBEMBE. Yoyodon is a better name –

BEN. oh yes – (Discreetly.) if you're illiterate –

OBEMBE. What did you say?

BEN (as Ikenna). *Our fishing line must be handled with pride and protection –*

OBEMBE. Ikenna was always serious.

BEN (as Ikenna). *On these iron hooks we will set our baits for the fishes.*

OBEMBE (*as Boja*). *Fish.*

BEN (*as Ikenna*). *Fishes – we will catch more than one!*

OBEMBE (*as Boja*). *What do you mean by baits Ikenna ?*

BEN (*as Ikenna*). *Boja, the baits are the prey or target to attract the fish to hinder themselves on our fishing hooks – worms, maggots, cockroaches, moths are all appealing treats for fishes – But don't go far – Father will obliterate me from existence if anything happens to any of you –*

(*They are at the river.*)

OBEMBE (*as Boja*). *Maybe there's a dead body part floating nearby –*

BEN (*as Ikenna*). *Why would you say such a thing?*

OBEMBE (*as Boja*). *Everybody knows – Omi-Ala is a cursed river –*

BEN (*as Ikenna*). *But it has good fishes –*

OBEMBE (*as Boja*). *That's because we don't reveal to the market traders where the catch has come from –*

BEN (*as Ikenna*). *That's just good business – you protect your source from market competition*

OBEMBE (*as Boja*). *What about the white-garment people?*

BEN (*as Ikenna*). *The Celestial Church? –*

OBEMBE (*as Boja*). *Water-spirit worshippers and their ritualistics –*

BEN (*as Ikenna*). *The town knows this is a pure river – it has served the town with pure water – People worshipped it for that –*

OBEMBE (*as Boja*). *Yes by praising the Orishas – Yemoja – Oshun and Osha –*

BEN (*as Ikenna*). *Before the Oyinbos came and changed people's feelings with their European Bible – but superstitious things are no longer relevant –*

OBEMBE (*as Boja*). *So that's why the white-garment church across the water are worshipping Yemoja – white is the colour of the Orisha –*

BEN (*as Ikenna*). *It's actually light blue –*

OBEMBE (*as Boja, excited*). *I have one on the line – Eja! Fish – It's a big one – I can't control it –*

BEN (*as Ikenna*). *Yes you can – Don't pull it – let it wriggle –*

OBEMBE (*as Boja*). *It's wriggling oooooh –*

BEN (*as Ikenna*). *Let it and when it wriggles towards you – take up the slack –*

OBEMBE (*as Boja*). *the slack? –*

BEN (*as Ikenna*). *On the fishing wire – like I taught you – reel it in –*

OBEMBE (*as Boja, reeling in the line as the fish jerks in and out of the water*). *Like this –*

BEN (*as Ikenna*). *Just like that – You're doing it – you see it's coming*

OBEMBE (*as Boja*). *It's a big one –*

BEN (*as Ikenna*). *Obembe, Ben grab the net – It's very jumpy –*

OBEMBE (*as Boja*). *Because it's caught – it knows it's caught – I have it!*

   (*Singing.*)
     Dance all you want –
     Fight all you will
     We have caught you
     You cannot escape
     Haven't we caught you
     You certainly can't escape
     We the fishermen have caught you –
     We the fishermen have caught you –
     You can't escape –

   (*As himself.*) Ikenna, there's a woman coming – It's Mama Iyabo –

BEN (*as Ikenna*). *What? – where?*

OBEMBE (*as Mama Iyabo*). *What is this? Why were you shouting like a pack of drunks?*

 Don't you know that the house of God is just on the other side?

 Don't you have any respect for God ehn?

BEN (*as Ikenna, rubbing his hands together*). *We are sorry Ma – We will refrain from shouting.*

OBEMBE (*as Mama Iyabo*). *What are you fishing from this river? Tadpoles – smelts – crabs – what?*

 Why don't you all go home –

BEN (*as Ikenna*). *Idiot –*

OBEMBE (*as Mama Iyabo*). *You dare call me names – Am I your age-mate?*

BEN (*as Ikenna*). *We already said we were sorry –*

OBEMBE (*as Mama Iyabo*). *Ah – to me you talk back – ah ah… well, it's your parents I pity –*

BEN (*as Ikenna*). *Save us your pity –*

OBEMBE (*as Mama Iyabo*). *I know you will be sorry if they found out you come here –*

BEN (*as Ikenna*). *What they don't know, won't hurt them or us so…*

OBEMBE (*as Mama Iyabo*). *Haven't you heard the government banned people from coming here – ohhoo kids of this generation –*

BEN (*as Ikenna*). *Elders of this generation –*

OBEMBE (*as Mama Iyabo, affronted*). *Ahhh… Whether you leave or not – do not raise your voices like that again –*

BEN (*laughing*). Did you smell her breath – I'm glad you made her stop talking Ikenna –

OBEMBE (*as Boja*). *She is so nosey – talking to us like vagabonds –*

BEN. adults are too judgemental –

OBEMBE (*as Boja*). *or just mental.* (*Laughing.*) *...Ike, what are you doing?*

BEN (*as Ikenna*). *I want to go home and study – I'm a student not a fisherman –*

OBEMBE (*as Boja*). *Now? – Isn't it too early and we have...*

BEN (*as Ikenna*). *Obembe, pack up the lines – Ben, pick up the cans and the rest of the bait.*

OBEMBE . Are we really leaving? Why are we going now? Is it because of Mama Iyabo or because of that time you met Abulu? Did I not tell you Abulu is just an evil crazy madman – Anyway you need blood sacrifice from an animal for a prophecy to come true – (*As Abulu.*) *Ikenna! Ikenna!*

BEN. Who is that?

OBEMBE. Abulu – he is the...

BEN. I know who Abulu is – Just wondering who was just speaking – who said that?

OBEMBE. Either Solomon or Kayode – they were both there as well –

BEN. I remember they were there – but which is it – Solomon or Kayode?

OBEMBE. Does it matter?

BEN. I think it does –

OBEMBE. Well let's say it's Kayode

BEN. because Solomon spoke in pidgin English –

OBEMBE. Okay – fine –

(*Silence.*)

3.

BEN. Ikenna's leadership – confusion upon confusion –

OBEMBE. Always unpredictable –

BEN. I never understood some of his actions – his decisions – always odd

OBEMBE. or not quite anticipated –

BEN. Peculiar older brother –

OBEMBE. Just for the record – we think the same about Ikenna –

BEN. we do –

OBEMBE. we do –

BEN. Good –

OBEMBE. Okay… sooooo

BEN. yes, so we're walking up the river path to the clearing – when Boja spotted –

BEN (*as Ikenna*). *You will see that Mama Iyabo will tell Mummy.*

OBEMBE (*as Boja*). *You don't know that. She's just a lonely widow.*

BEN (*as Ikenna*). *A widow that when her husband died in Sierra Leone – Mummy was her main helper. She is forever indebted to Mummy.*

OBEMBE. I remember we didn't go fishing the next day. Or the day after.

BEN. Or the one after the one after the one after that.

OBEMBE. For a long time – yes… no fishing –

BEN. We would just sit in our rooms – do homework – pray –

OBEMBE. And wait – Wait for Mother to return –

BEN. Soon Solomon came to find out why we had not been coming to the river –

OBEMBE (*as Solomon*). *Oh boy – you dey get fear for fishing now abi? Why you and your brothers no dey come again?*

BEN (*as Ikenna*). *It's too risky and that river has some supernatural juju for perimeter*

OBEMBE (*as Solomon*). *Nonsense you dey talk –*

BEN (*as Ikenna*). *Solomon – you know me – I no get threat – I no dey scare easy for skin – but, Omi-Ala no be fit for play – It no fit me and my brothers to play there self –*

OBEMBE (*as Solomon*). *So you really no dey catch for market again – na so you waste my time learning you expert fishing?*

BEN (*as Ikenna*). *I beg no be vex – make we expand your enterprise – Our fishing equipment take for extra catch –*

OBEMBE (*as Solomon*). *Your equipment no fit suit my own – I get plenty better fish hooks and nets –*

BEN (*as Ikenna*). *You know fit sell am –*

OBEMBE (*as Solomon, laughing*). *Who go buy am? Na fishing time and catch money I go lose if I take am for sell – Na wa for you o – Na your own be that one – I go see you around sha –*

BEN. We would just sit in our rooms

OBEMBE. and wait… for Mother to return.

(*Silence.*)

BEN (*as Mother*). *You don't deserve to eat anything from this house – Go and eat the fish you caught from the dangerous river and be stuffed by it – I will tell Eme what you have done – (Snaps her fingers.) You think I would have ceased to exist if something bad had happened to you? – If one of you had drowned in that river? I will not cease to live because you chose to harm yourselves – no ami kor – Proverbs Chapter Thirty, Verse Seventeen – The eyes that mocks a father – that scorns an aged mother will be plucked out by the ravens of the valley – will be eaten by the vultures –*

OBEMBE (*as Boja*). *We are sorry Mama – we were not thinking – Ikenna and I understand you are angry with us – but please do not tell Father – we realise the river has nothing for us –*

BEN (*as Mother*). *Boja, you should have thought of that before your transgression –*

OBEMBE (*as Boja*). *We will not do anything wrong again –*

BEN (*as Mother*). *Tell it to your father –*

(*Silence. They sit.*)

(*As Ikenna.*) *We have to destroy all the fishing paraphernalia –*

OBEMBE (*as Boja*). *We can't burn them – the smoke would be visible for miles*

BEN (*as Ikenna*). *We will hide and then discard them slowly in time –*

OBEMBE (*as Boja*). *Obembe and I will hide the tins and fishing hooks*

BEN (*as Ikenna*). *Where will you hide them?*

OBEMBE (*as Boja*). *At the back of Mummy's tomato garden*

BEN (*as Ikenna*). *Not in the soil –*

OBEMBE (*as Boja*). *No not there / Mummy could find them –*

BEN (*as Ikenna*). *Mummy will find them –*

OBEMBE (*as Boja*). *I know – I thought that –*

BEN (*as Ikenna*). *but where?*

OBEMBE (*as Boja*). *under the rusting roofing sheets the builders left when they built the house –*

BEN (*as Ikenna*). *Good idea –*

(*Silence.*)

OBEMBE. Father visited on the Saturday – it was exactly five days after we were caught

BEN. Yes – You and I believed God could touch Father's heart and prevent him from whipping us –

OBEMBE (*fervently*). Lord Jesus – You say you love us – Don't allow Father to visit again.

BEN. Let him stay in Yola

OBEMBE. Please Jesus.

BEN. You know how hard he would whip us – Lord don't you even know –

OBEMBE. tell him

BEN. Please listen Jesus – If you let him come back and whip us –

OBEMBE. We won't go to Sunday school again –

BEN. And we won't sing

OBEMBE. And clap

BOTH. In church

OBEMBE. Ever again

BOTH. Amen –

BEN. Then Ikenna came in.

OBEMBE. I thought it was Boja?

BEN. It was Ikenna – he was the mastermind of the operation.

OBEMBE. Yes, that's very true.

BEN (*as Ikenna*). *When Father arrives – We will remain in our bedroom and pretend to be asleep. Are we all agreed?*

OBEMBE. Agreed.

(*Silence.*)

4.

BEN (*as Ikenna*). *Where is he now?*

OBEMBE. Kitchen I think… No living room – What are they talking about?

BEN. Erm… Father's job – money… Apparently the naira is going down in value under the current government… Now… I think it's politics –

OBEMBE. How do you know?

BEN. Father just switched to English – He just said 'ministration'.

OBEMBE (*as Father*). *Nnamdi Azikiwe is in hospital in Enugu – Zik might die because of the poor facilities… Can you imagine the first President of this so-called great Nigerian nation toiling towards his demise watching a country he strived to unify still marginalising us Igbos – his own people still struggling for equality after the disastrous Biafra – Abacha is an ignoramus – The British knew they were creating a monster with their ill-considered amalgamation –*

BEN (*as Mother*). *Dim – there's something I want to tell you –*

OBEMBE (*as Father*). *I'm all ears*

BEN (*as Mother*). *Dim – Your sons – Ikene, Boja, Obembe and Benjamin – have done the worst, the very unimaginable worst –*

OBEMBE (*as Father*). *What have they done?*

BEN (*as Mother*). *Aie, Dim – Do you know Mama Iyabo – Yuseef's wife – the one who sells groundnut –*

OBEMBE (*as Father*). *Yes yes I know her – go straight to what they did my friend*

BEN (*as Mother*). *Eheeeh – let me land… Dim, that woman was selling groundnut to that old priest of the Celestial Church close to the Omi-Ala, when she saw the boys fishing – she recognised them at once –*

(*A despicable silence.*)

OBEMBE (*as Father*). *Adako – that dangerous river under a curfew – where even adults are known to have disappeared –*

BEN (*as Mother*). *Eheeeh – It was your sons she saw –*

OBEMBE (*as Father*). *Gray-shious – Me – Gray-shious – Me – So you really mean it was my boys –*

BEN (*as Mother*). *They are all inside – Just ask them and you will see for yourself – To think they actually bought fishing equipment – hooks – lines and sinkers – With the pocket money you gave them –*

OBEMBE (*as Father*). *Ahhhh – Gray-shious – Me – Implicating me in their treachery – How long did they do this?*

BEN....

OBEMBE (*as Father*). *Am I talking to myself – You are not deaf and mute –*

BEN (*as Mother*). *Three weeks? –*

OBEMBE (*as Father*). *Good gracious Adako – Three weeks? With you under the same roof?*

   IKENNA... IKE – NNA

BEN (*as Mother*). *BOJA! OBEMBE! BENJAMIN!*

OBEMBE (*as Father*). *IKENNA!*

BEN (*as Ikenna*)....*Sir?*

OBEMBE (*as Father*). *Come out here at once! Now...I suppose you all heard what your mother has told me – Is it true?*

BEN (*as Ikenna*). *It is true sir*

OBEMBE (*as Father*). *I sweat and suffer to send you to school to receive a good Western education as civilised men, but you chose instead to be fishermen? Fish – ah – men? Fish – ah – men? Fish – ah – men? Ikenna big for nothing – spread*

*for me kia kia – Spread! (To Mother.) Adako, if you intervene
– You will count out your own blows along with these
senseless insolent boys!*

(Father beats Ikenna.)

BEN. I don't know if he meant it – Ikenna received twenty hard
blows. Boja counted fifteen. You and I received eight apiece.
He used the cow hides – Kobokos from the meat-roasting
Malam. That one is very painful.

OBEMBE *(as Father, hand on chin, staring at the boys). Now
listen all of you – Your mother and I are appalled by the
dangerous risks you took – Nowhere around that deadly
river will you find books to read – Do you no longer have
eyes for your books? Let me warn you my friends – If any of
you enters this house – with a bad school report – I will send
you to your grandmother's village to farm or tap palm
wine –*

BEN *(as Mother, snapping fingers over her head). Tufia – God
forbid – None of my children will fail, to then go and toil the
land –*

OBEMBE *(as Father). Yes – God forbid – How will God
forbid? – You shop closing time is now five – No longer
seven and no work on Saturdays – I can't have our children
sliding into the pits of delinquency under your nose whilst I
am in a different state in the country – No one enjoys beating
his children – no one… On the other hand, even though what
you did was wrong – It reflected that you have the courage to
indulge in something adventurous – Such adventurous spirit
is the spirit of men – So from now on I want you to channel
that spirit into something more fruitful – I want you to be a
different kind of fishermen – Not the kind of fishermen that
fish at a river like Omi-Ala – but fishermen of the mind – go-
gettas – children who will dip their hands into rivers and
seize oceans of this life and become successful – become
doctors, pilots, professors – laywers ehn – those are the kind
of fishermen I want as children – juggernauts – juggernauts
– Boja – Ikenna are you following –*

BEN (*as Ikenna*). *Yes sir –*

OBEMBE (*as Father*). *Menacing – unstoppable fishermen – menacing – unstoppable fishermen – fishermen of dreams – you will now recite an anthem… follow me… We trail behind our lines –*

BEN (*as Ikenna*). *We trail behind our lines.*

OBEMBE (*as Father*). *Hook line and sinkers.*

BEN (*as Ikenna*). *Hook line and sinkers.*

OBEMBE (*as Father*). *We are fishermen.*

BEN (*as Ikenna*). *We are fishermen.*

BOTH. *Fishermen*

(*Father laughs.*)

OBEMBE (*as Father*). *Now will the born-again fishermen embrace me? Ike? Do you know why I flogged you the most?*

BEN (*as Ikenna*). *Yes.*

OBEMBE (*as Father*). *Why?*

BEN (*as Ikenna*). *Because I am the first-born – their leader.*

OBEMBE (*as* Father). *Good – Bear that in mind – from now on before you take any action – look at them – they do whatever you do – and go wherever you go – that's to their credit – so Ikenna don't lead your brothers astray –*

BEN (*as Ikenna*). *Yes Daddy –*

OBEMBE (*as Father*). *Guide them well –*

BEN (*as Ikenna*). *Yes Daddy –*

OBEMBE (*as Father*). *Lead them well – Always remember that a coconut that falls into a cistern will need a good washing before it can be eaten – do you hear?*

BEN (*as Ikenna*). *I hear sir –*

OBEMBE (*as Father*). *And you have been corrected –*

BEN (*as Ikenna*). *Yes sir* –

OBEMBE (*as Father*). *Do you promise?*

BEN (*as Ikenna*). *I promise* –

OBEMBE. Father left again for Yola on the Sunday –

BEN. Ikenna changed after the beating –

OBEMBE. He was hot-tempered and wanted revenge –

BEN (*as Ikenna*). *We must punish Mama Iyabo – she told on us and I will have my pound of flesh* –

OBEMBE. I don't think that's a good idea –

BEN (*as Ikenna*). *You must all help me, because you caused us to get caught – had you listened to me she would not have caused Father to beat me so much – look – just look – (Pulls down his shorts to shows his whip marks.) at my buttocks* –

OBEMBE (*as Boja*). *Aishhhhh, Ikenna! Sorry Ooooo!* –

BEN (*as Ikenna*). *That is what you and that idiotic woman caused me – so you all should come up with ideas on how to punish her – (Snapping his fingers.) We must do that today – that way she will know she cannot mess with us and go scot-free – Boja?*

OBEMBE (*as Boja relaxed*). *okay… you know Mama Iyabo has lots of chickens – yes she keeps a whole lot* –

So I am thinking we get in their compound and set the hens free –

BEN (*as Ikenna*). *that is fatal… But I don't think we can get away with it without those birds making noise – she will hear or suspect it was us, which will earn us even more severe strokes of Father's whip – None of us want that – Obembe what's your idea?*

OBEMBE. What if we throw stones – maybe large ones – boulders – into her compound and we pray they hit her or one of her sons –

BEN (*as Ikenna*). *Wrong idea – what if those big hungry sons of her – those Hulk Hogan lookalikes will catch and beat us? –*

OBEMBE (*as Boja*). *Yes, they will beat us even worse than Father – no mercy*

BEN. What if? –

OBEMBE (*as Boja*). *Ben, what do you have to say?*

BEN. I have an idea –

OBEMBE (*as Boja*). *Then say it –*

BEN. Okay okay – I suggest we get one of the chickens and... and...

OBEMBE (*as Boja*). *Yes?*

BEN. Behead it –

OBEMBE. (*Clapping*). *That is really fatal – Oh boy yaeeeee – that idea surprised even me –*

BEN. Mama Iyabo lived in the small bungalow compound –

OBEMBE. It was identical to our own – the small balcony – two windows –

BEN. Blue windows and doors –

OBEMBE. But her fence was mud and clay –

BEN. Ours was bricks and cement –

5.

BEN (*as Ikenna*). *Can you see them?*

OBEMBE (*as Boja*). *They are everywhere just pecking their way through the dry grass –*

BEN (*as Ikenna*). *Let's not waste any time – We don't want to take too long – let's quietly catch one –*

(*They stalk the hens.*)

OBEMBE (*as Boja*). *I have one –*

BEN (*as Ikenna*). *Don't let it go – Don't let it go – That's my boy – that's my boy... Yes this is a good spot we can cover the blood with dust –*

OBEMBE (*as Boja*). *Do you want the knife?*

BEN (*as Ikenna*). *Yes give it to me – Boja hold its head and the body – show me its neck –*

OBEMBE (*as Boja*). *You'll have to be quick – it wants to fly –*

BEN (*as Ikenna*). *I'll slit its throat and put a stop to it –*

OBEMBE (*as Boja*). *Obembe hold its feet – I can feel it twitching – Ben don't you want to look – Ahh ha, you are shaking your head –*

(*Silence.*)

BEN (*as Ikenna*). *There it is done –*

OBEMBE (*as Boja*). *Shall I throw it over now?*

BEN (*as Ikenna*). *take it by the feet –*

OBEMBE. The chicken's blood was trailing all the way back to Mama Iyabo's house –

BEN. Ibafe's grandfather saw us and looked astonished –

OBEMBE. No one would believe the senile old man

BEN (*as Ikenna*). *On the count of three –*

OBEMBE (*as Boja*). *One –*

BEN (*as Ikenna*). *Two –*

BOTH. *Three –*

(*Boja launches the decapitated chicken over the fence into Mama Iyabo's compound.*)

OBEMBE (*as Boja*)....*Done –*

BEN (*as Ikenna*). *Good… We've had our revenge –*

OBEMBE. Ben, what's wrong?

BEN. We could have stopped it –

OBEMBE. How? Ikenna was determined –

BEN. But maybe if we convinced him –

6.

OBEMBE. After that – Ikenna remained in his room the whole time – Two days and we didn't even see him – he just stayed in his room – no one, not even Boja who he shared his room with could enter –

BEN. I remember Boja was upset at not being allowed into their room –

OBEMBE (*as Boja*). *Ikenna has to be stopped – this cannot continue – Ikenna has lost his mind – he has gone mad – Mosquitoes nearly killed me last night – I'm tired of what Ikenna is doing to me – Can you imagine? – To be so righteous to expel me from my own room – the room Mummy and Daddy gave both of us – I hate him for this –*

(*Silence.*)

BEN (*as Ikenna, softly*). *Did you say you hate me?… Did you say it or not?*

OBEMBE (*as Boja*). *Yes, yes I hate you, Ike, I do –*

BEN (*as Ikenna*). *You hate me, Boja?* (*Smiling and nodding.*) *I knew it, I knew it – I have only been foolish all this while –* (*Shaking his head.*) *I have dreamed of you chasing me with a gun –*

OBEMBE (*as Boja*). *What has that got to do with anything?*

BEN (*as Ikenna*). *So I know my spirit attests to how much you hate me – I knew Abulu saw that vision that you were the fisherman he talked about – nobody else – That's why I'm not surprised when you now confess that you hate me – you always have – but you will not succeed.*

OBEMBE (*as Abulu*). *Ikenna! Ikenna!*

   (*Silence.*)

7.

OBEMBE. Does Mummy still make Eba and Ogbono soup?

BEN. You always remember food.

OBEMBE. I like food and Mummy's was the best.

BEN. I don't want to think about food right now.

OBEMBE. I loved Mummy's food –

BEN. Yes I know – You always fall asleep straight away –

OBEMBE. Brother you mustn't deprive yourself of the pleasures of life –

BEN. Some things just didn't taste the same after –

OBEMBE. I loved it when she called me king – I would go soft and give in to her request.

BEN. You were supposed to stay strong and not say anything – like Ikenna told us. You just spilled the secret like a broken calabash.

OBEMBE. It was Mummy – our mother – the mother of all mothers – what was I meant to do?

BEN (*as Mother*). *Wake up – Wake up – It's me – do you hear – It's me?*

OBEMBE....Yes Mama –

BEN (*as Mother*). *I want to ask both of you something... Eh heh – Listen I want you to tell me what caused this rift between Boja and Ikenna – I'm sure both of you know and I want you to tell me quick! – quick! –*

OBEMBE. Mummy, I don't know

BEN (*as Mother*). *Tell me what happened between your brothers – Did they have a fight?*

OBEMBE. No

BEN (*as Mother*). *So what happened – tell me – Eh – My princes, Obembe Igwe, My King, Azikiwe, gwa nu ife me lu mu biko my husbands –*

OBEMBE. [It began the day] we met Abulu at Omi-Ala –

BEN (*as Mother*). *Eh – Abulu the madman – Chineke!*

OBEMBE. Mummy not so loud! –

BEN (*as Mother*). *Tell me at once what happened when you met him – Do you hear me, Obembe? I'm saying it for the last time – Tell me what happened at that river –*

OBEMBE....We had just completed a fishing session at the river and were walking home when our friend Solomon shouted – (*As Solomon.*) *Look self – One dead man for under tree – A dead man –*

BEN (*as Ikenna*). *How can a dead man be humming song – That is not a dead man – he must be a madman – that is how mad people behave –*

OBEMBE. It was Kayode that recognised the madman – (*As Kayode.*) *Ikenna is right – That is Abulu – The vision-seeing madman – (Snaps his fingers.) I detest this man – It is him for sure – Abulu*

BEN (*as Ikenna*). *I did not even recognise him with clothes on – Boja you see him?*

OBEMBE (*as Boja*). *I see him – Look, he is moving –*

BEN (*as Ikenna*). *Look how mechanical and straight he sits up – I think he is entranced – he's no longer of this earth – Let's leave him alone and go on our way – Let's not talk to him – he mustn't see us – Let's just go quick quick –*

OBEMBE (*as Boja*). *No, no, we should rattle him a bit – It will be fun – Just one time – We shouldn't just leave like that – We should frighten him –*

BEN (*as Ikenna*). *No – Are you mad? Don't you know this man is evil? Don't you know him?*

OBEMBE (*as Abulu, laughing*). *Ikenna… Ikenna… Ikenna*

BEN. Let's go home now – let's go – It's not good to listen to Abulu Ike – Let us go –

OBEMBE (*as Abulu, softly*). *Ikenna – (Sings 'The Sower of Green Things'.) Ikenna, you will be bound like a bird on the day you shall die – Ikenna, you will be mute – Ikenna, you will be crippled – You tongue will stick out of your mouth like a hungry beast and will not return back into your mouth – Ikenna you shall lift your hands to grasp air, but you will not be able to breathe, Ikenna, you shall open mouth to speak on that day… ah, ah – but words will freeze in your mouth.*

(*An aeroplane flies overhead.*)

BEN. The din of an aircraft over our heads swallowed the rest of Abulu's words –

(*Once again we hear Abulu singing 'The Sower of Green Things'.*)

(*As Ikenna.*) *…Did any of you hear what he said when the plane flew over our heads?*

OBEMBE.…I did –

BEN (*as Ikenna*). *What then are you waiting for?… Are you deaf? Tell me –*

OBEMBE.…He said, he said, he said – He said that a fisherman will kill you Ike –

BEN (*as Ikenna*). *Are you sure? How did he say it? His words exactly*

OBEMBE. He said – (*Impersonating Abulu.*) …*Ikenna, you shall… Ikenna, you shall die by the hands of a fisherman – Ikenna you will swim in a river of red but shall never rise.*

BEN (*as Ikenna, looks at his brothers*)….*He saw a vision that one of you will kill me –*

OBEMBE. But I don't want to kill you Ike –

BEN (*as himself*). You did not say that –

OBEMBE. I distinctly remember my own words –

BEN. None us said anything after Ikenna accused us – I wanted to respond but nothing came out –

OBEMBE….I remember Ikenna just walked away and we just followed him home quietly –

BEN. That night I had a dream that we were in our grandparents' village in Igboland – the four of us were playing football and Boja took a big kick and cleared the ball to the remaining old Biafran bridge to help the family escape towards Cameroon should the Nigerian forces attack – held together by wooden slats – rope and metal hooks – no handrails for support – the river underneath was bedded with many rocks and stones – Ikenna without thinking quickly ran on to the bridge to collect the ball from the middle of the bridge – only when he had the ball in his hand did he realise he was in danger – Ikenna began to shout and cry – help – help – the three of us saw his fear and began calling him – Ikenna – come – come – Ikenna – quickly let the ball fall – spread his hands and started walking towards us – as he made his way towards us – the binding snapped and the slats became loose – Ikenna lost his footing and descended with the decrepit bridge particles – shouting for help – he was still falling when I was abruptly woken by you shouting –

8.

OBEMBE. Wake up – Wake up Ben – they are quarrelling –

BEN. What – who?

OBEMBE. Ikenna and Boja – It's a serious argument – It is fierce, come

(They rush to observe at a distance in the hallway.)

BEN *(as Ikenna)*. *Why do you want to disturb me from my sleep?* –

OBEMBE *(as Boja)*. *Ikenna – You'd better open the door right now – the room is mine too – I'm ready for you – If this is what you want, come out to the open space in the backyard, so we don't destroy anything in the house – so Mummy will not find out what happened*

BEN *(as Ikenna)*. *Shut up – You think you can take me? Just remember, you started this* –

(Ikenna and Boja begin to scuffle.)

OBEMBE. I couldn't believe our elder brothers were actually fighting –

BEN. They were not playing – Ikenna broke Boja's nose and blood started to pour on to his blue shirt

OBEMBE. You began to cry –

BEN. As did you –

OBEMBE. Yes, I was also crying and we knew there was only one solution –

BEN. Obembe, we need to get an adult to separate them

OBEMBE. Let's go quickly quickly –

BEN. the house of the next-door neighbour –

OBEMBE. they travelled two days ago –

BEN. Look – *(Pointing.)* Pastor Collins

OBEMBE. In the church van –

    (*They both wave to no avail.*)

BEN. He didn't see us –

OBEMBE. Someone else –

BEN. We found Mr Bode –

OBEMBE. The motor mechanic – Good afternoon sir –

BEN (*as Mr Bode*). *Boys – How are you?*

OBEMBE. We are fine sir –

BEN (*as Mr Bode*). *What can I do for you boys?* –

OBEMBE. Yes sir – Our brothers are fighting –

BEN. They are bleeding – eje yen ti po ju – too much blood –
    Please come and help –

OBEMBE. We need an adult to stop them – they are too strong
    for us – they will only listen to an adult

BEN (*as Mr Bode*). *What kind of thing is this – Why are they
    fighting?*

OBEMBE. We don't know sir – Please help –

BEN (*as Mr Bode*). *Okay – let's go* –

OBEMBE. We ran ahead –

BEN. We looked for them around the compound –

OBEMBE. We could not see them

BEN (*as Mr Bode*). *Where have they gone? – Where did you
    say they were fighting?* –

OBEMBE. Right here sir – here, on this spot –

BEN (*as Mr Bode*). *Are you sure?*

OBEMBE. Yes sir – here, right here in the backyard is where
    we left them – here – here – they were fighting here – see the
    blood in the dirt – And their torn garments –

BEN (*as Mr Bode*). *Then where might they be?… okay, let us go back inside the house –*

It is well – let's go – they've stopped fighting

OBEMBE. We were relieved –

BEN. Boja! Ikenna! You and Mr Bode entered the house calling –

OBEMBE. Mummy's chair was broken at the arm and its feet were bent backwards – I stood beside Mr Bode –

BEN. Mr Bode stood beside you with his arms on his head –

OBEMBE. Our brother was facing the radiator – his eyes wide open and fixed into one place –

His tongue was out of his mouth and white foam trailed down to the floor – River of red

(OBEMBE *repeats 'river of red' throughout*.)

BEN. His hands were wide apart and sticking out of Ikenna's belly was the wooden end of Mummy's kitchen knife – its sharp blade was deep in his flesh – The floor was drenched in his blood… (*Similar to Abulu's pronunciation*.) Ikenna! Ikenna! Ikenna!.

OBEMBE. It came true –

BEN (*as Abulu*). *Ikenna!*

OBEMBE. Stop! I don't want to do this any more.

(*Silence*.)

9.

BEN. Ikenna's body disappeared in an ambulance to the General Hospital.

OBEMBE. Neighbours tried to comfort us with words –

BEN (*as neighbours*). *Ejo ema sukun mon oma'da – Do not weep, it will be well*

OBEMBE. I heard Mummy make a phone call to Daddy a few hours after Ikenna was found –

BEN (*as Mother, anguished*). *Eme, Ikenna naaaaa!*

OBEMBE. I had never heard a sound like that from Mummy – Daddy returned with all his things with no intention of leaving again –

BEN. Ikenna's funeral happened in four days as if we subscribed to Islamic practice –

OBEMBE. Relatives came from the village Amano – do you remember?

BEN. Of course I do –

OBEMBE. Cousins – uncles – aunties –

BEN. relatives we did not remember and many we had never met – dressed in black – with familiar features resembled our brother separately –

OBEMBE. Ikenna was dressed differently in sparkling white shirt and trousers –

BEN. He had the glow of an angel as Mummy cried and beat her breast while she was being restrained by Daddy and our aunties… Pastor Collins prayed loudly to suppress Mama's howl –

OBEMBE (*as Pastor Collins*)….*that you forgive and receive his soul into your kingdom – we know that in the same way you gave, you have taken, and we are challenged with the fortitude to bear the loss – thank you Lord Jesus for we know, it is all in you plan and you have heard us –*

(*Silence.*)

OBEMBE. I changed after Ikenna's funeral –

BEN. you were planning something I could tell –

OBEMBE. You couldn't tell – I was what Father would call stoic – placid – he would say placid

BEN. you were never placid – you were the other p – pensive – even perturbed

OBEMBE. Ben our brother had just been buried – I wasn't sleeping from nightmares – guilt and thinking I was inept, so forgive me if I wasn't doing kick-ups or spying on our neighbour's daughter in the outside shower –

BEN. I saw you –

OBEMBE. when? what do you mean? When?

BEN....I just saw you –

OBEMBE. Was I invisible before? –

BEN. Of course not –

OBEMBE. So what did you see?

BEN. kneeling in Mummy's tomato garden –

OBEMBE. harvesting –

BEN. You were distraught –

OBEMBE. Rotten tomatoes –

BEN. You swore at God – You condemned God and renounced your faith –

OBEMBE. It wasn't fair – we were cheated – it made no sense

(*Silence.*)

BEN....[It didn't]

OBEMBE. it hurt –

(*Silence.*)

10.

OBEMBE. Boja Agwu, fourteen was last seen at his house –

BEN. 21 Araromi Street, High School Road, Akure, August 4th 1996 –

OBEMBE. Wearing a faded blue T-shirt with an image of Bahamas beach –

BEN. T-shirt was bloodstained and torn when last seen – Please if seen kindly report to your nearest police station –

OBEMBE. He did not cry out when his photo streamed across televisions in Akure –

BEN. Taking up air time on OSRC and NTA channels –

OBEMBE. He just decided to appear in our dreams at night-time and as figments of Mummy's imagination –

BEN. Mummy always says when Boja was born it was on the bed she shared with Daddy – she lost so much blood that it seeped through the mattress and formed a permanent stain underneath the bed –

OBEMBE. Daddy tried to remain patient with the police – give them time to do their job

BEN. But two hours after Ikenna's funeral, Daddy took me along with him to the police station –

OBEMBE (*as Father*). *Can I see the deputy police officer?*

BEN (*as Officer*). *Can you identify yourself sirrrrrr?*

OBEMBE (*as Father*). *I'm Mr James Agwu – A staff member of the Central Bank of Nigeria –*

(*Father reaches into his breast pocket and presents the police officer with a red ID card.*

Officer hands back the card.)

BEN (*as Officer*). *Oga – You go do us well abi – You know say na you be Oga at the top – Our palm is not a stretch for your pocket abi –*

OBEMBE (*as Father*). *Your ridiculous insinuation is why this country will not prosper – I don't have time for this – My child is missing – can you conscientiously do your so-called job*

BEN (*as Officer*). *Ah! – So you are the father of those boys – sorry for that sir – Please sit down… Erm Mr Agwu – I regret to say that we are yet to have a word on the location of your son – but we have been making progress – We questioned someone in your neighbourhood who confirms she saw the boy across the street that afternoon –*

OBEMBE (*as Father*). *Which direction did she say he went?*

BEN (*as Officer*). *We don't know for now but we – members of our team – (Coughs.)*

OBEMBE (*as Father*). *E'Pele – Sorry*

BEN (*as Officer*). *Thank you – But you know even that will be futile, if we don't attach a ransom soon – Primarily, it is meant to involve the people of this town – With money on the ground, I'm sure people will be keen to respond – If not, our efforts will be similar to sweeping the streets with a broom at night – ill sight will mean the dust will just lay wait and obscure the effort –*

OBEMBE (*as Father*). *I understand what you're saying Deputy Officer, but I want to trust my instincts on this matter and wait for your preliminary search to be completed, before I go on with any personal plans of my own –*

(*Officer nods rapidly.*)

OBEMBE (*as Father*). *Something tells me he's safe somewhere – Boja is merely hiding because of what he did –*

BEN (*as Officer*). *Yes… (Uneasy in his seat.) You know a child and sometimes adults, having done such a terrible thing – I mean after killing his blood brother, he would be afraid – He might be afraid of us the police, or even you, his parents – of the future – of everything – there's even a chance he may have left the town entirely –*

OBEMBE (*as Father*). *Yes – (Shaking his head.)*

BEN (*as Officer*). *That reminds me – have you tried to reach any of your relatives in nearby places to ask –*

OBEMBE (*as Father*). *Yes – but I don't think this is likely – rarely do we visit our relatives – so he wouldn't know where to go –*

BEN (*as Officer*). *I understand your point – we will do our best – But we hope he returns by himself in his own time –*

OBEMBE (*as Father*). *We hope too – thank you… for your effort DPO*

(*Officer extends his hand out, expectant of a bribe, but Father just shakes the Officer's outstretched hand and leaves.*)

11.

BEN. Boja revealed himself soon after Father and I returned from the police station.

Our neighbour Mrs Abati just started to scream –

OBEMBE (*as Mrs Abati*). *Awoooooo – Awooooo – Awoooooo – He is in the well ohhh – Awooooo – There – there in the well – In the water – looking at me –*

BEN. Father wouldn't let us near the well –

OBEMBE. I wanted to go so bad – to see –

BEN. His head was above water rested against the wall of the well

OBEMBE. and his hands were reaching out as if holding off an invisible attack –

BEN. The well had killed him – he drowned – it was the water –

OBEMBE. Mr Bode climbed down the well – he tried to pull Boja out of the water with one arm – but Boja's death-heavy body slipped back down into the water

BEN. The people helping –

OBEMBE. Spectating, useless gossips –

BEN. Passed down a ladder to Mr Bode –

OBEMBE. The ladder was already in with him when he first went down –

BEN. How do you know – you weren't there –

OBEMBE. Neither were you – You were next to me on the balcony

BEN. …Okay the ladder was already in the well – in the water –

OBEMBE. Wait – what did he even need a ladder for –

BEN. For a lot of things –

OBEMBE. Like what?

BEN. Leverage – to create a track from Boja's body to follow –

OBEMBE. ooooh ooooo –

BEN. They hoisted Boja's body out of the well

OBEMBE. The crowd of people cheered –

BEN. It was a roar –

OBEMBE. You hear what I hear – did we not both hear?

BEN. Different sounds – I was on the balcony

OBEMBE. Me too –

BEN. [I know] – we were both on the balcony –

OBEMBE. Next to each other –

BEN. Father found us on the balcony –

OBEMBE (*as Father*). *You both – Inside – On the sofa…*

BEN. His face had fresh wrinkles and his eyes were bloodshot –

OBEMBE. I remember what he said –

BEN. So do I –

OBEMBE. Word for word? –

BEN. Try me –

OBEMBE. Okay –

BEN. You as well –

OBEMBE. Together?–

BEN. Are you sure? –

OBEMBE. Just let me hear you –

BEN. Go! –

BOTH (*as Father*). *From this moment on – both of you will be strong men – you will be men who will look into the eyes of the world and order your ways and paths through it – with – with the sort of courage your brothers had… do you understand?*

(BOTH *nod*.)

OBEMBE (*as Father, nodding*).*…good… Jesus – Now that this has happened – Obembe you have to drive your younger brother – you will be looked up to as the elder brother now – I am not saying you should drive in the car o – I mean you just lead – lead him – show Ben the way – Do you hear Ben? Listen and follow the lead of your elder brother Obembe – Ben?*

BEN. Okay Daddy –

(*Silence*.)

12.

OBEMBE. Do you know that we drank the blood from his wounds –

BEN (*shaking his head*). [That's not true.]

OBEMBE. Listen, don't you know anything? Did you not know that there was a big hole in his head – and we made tea with the well water – we all drank from it –

BEN....

OBEMBE. Because he was there –

BEN. If he was there – there –

OBEMBE. Go on –

BEN. If he was there –

OBEMBE. Say it –

BEN. if he was there – how did we not see him all that time –

OBEMBE. Because when something drowns – it doesn't come up straight away – remember the lizard that fell into Kayode's water drum – and it bloated and came up – it happens that way – (*Points outside.*) it happens that way –

(BEN *vomits*.)

Water – let me get you some water –

BEN. I watched them load Boja's body into the ambulance from the sitting-room window – making sure Father did not see me –

OBEMBE. When the ambulance started to drive off

BEN. You hugged me –

OBEMBE. Ben –

BEN. ehn –

OBEMBE. Ike and Boja are dead –

BEN. ...

OBEMBE. I'll clean up –

(*Silence.*)

13.

BEN. Two nights after Mummy returned from hospital, we were in our bedroom –

OBEMBE. Ben – Listen, I just – I just remembered in a book I once read – I don't remember the name but it was written by an Igbo man – You see – the people of Umuofia were conquered because there were not united – The white men were a common enemy that would have been easily conquered if the tribe had fought as one – Do you see why our brothers died?

BEN. I don't know –

OBEMBE. The same way – because there was a division between them –

BEN. ...Yes –

OBEMBE. But do you know why Ike and Boja were divided? – Abulu's prophecy – because of Abulu's prophecy – Abulu killed our brothers – He is our enemy... I will kill Abulu –

BEN. ...Why would you do that?

OBEMBE. I will do it for them – I want to do it for our brothers

BEN. why are you locking the door and closing the window? –

OBEMBE. To prevent God from seeing our plot –

(*Silence.*

OBEMBE *strikes a match and lights a cigarette.*)

BEN. You are smoking now?

OBEMBE. It's what you do – when the stress of the world gets to you –

BEN. In our bedroom?

(BEN *begins to walk out*.)

OBEMBE. Are you going to tell Mummy and Daddy? – Go – but if I die at their hands – I will come back to Earth and haunt you –

(*Silence*.

OBEMBE *goes to the window*.)

BEN. Obe… Obe – But why must you kill the madman?

OBEMBE. It is simple Ben – I want to kill him because he killed my brothers and so does not deserve to live –

BEN. But to *kill* a person – it's not easy

OBEMBE. Abulu is walking around mocking us as if our family means nothing – As if we mean nothing to no one –

BEN. But must we try to kill the demon-man? Is there no other way Obe?

OBEMBE. No – listen, if you and I were not too scared to interfere when they were fighting until they killed each other – We must not be afraid to avenge them now – We must kill Abulu or else we cannot have peace – I cannot have peace – Daddy and Mummy cannot have peace – Mummy was driven crazy because of that madman – She is still not herself – He has inflicted a wound on us that will never heal – Do you agree?

BEN….

(*Silence*.)

OBEMBE. You are still not convinced – Where's Daddy?

BEN. He had gone to the far far petrol station on the way out of Akure, because the government increased petrol prices from – (*As Father.*) *twelve naira to twenty-one naira* – (*As himself.*) [Daddy was disgusted] –

(*Silence.*)

14.

OBEMBE. Daddy hated Mummy's silence –

BEN. He made excuses to leave the house to drink palm wine –

OBEMBE. He was drunk a lot – you could smell it but he didn't stagger –

BEN. I think he felt threatened –

OBEMBE. In what way?

BEN. The silence made him afraid of her –

OBEMBE. Mummy eventually gave in –

BEN (*as Mother*). *Eme! Eme! I felt Boja standing in the kitchen while I cooked.*

OBEMBE (*as Father*). *Just how my friend?*

BEN (*as Mother*). *How dare you say this to me Eme? – how dare you? – Am I not the mother of these children? Can I not know when their spirits disturb me? You can pretend you are not listening to me but you cannot pretend children die the way they should have. Eme you and I know they didn't – just go out and see – Eme Eme – it isn't normal – parents shouldn't bury their children – it should be the other way around.*

(*Silence.*)

Eme – Do you see the white cow grazing here?

OBEMBE (*as Father*). *What? – What cow?*

BEN (*as Mother, laughing*). *Can't you see the cow eating the grass there?*

OBEMBE (*as Father*). *Which cow my friend?*

BEN (*as Mother*). *Eme have you gone blind – you can't see the shiny white cow no?*

BEN. I couldn't believe it – I thought it was possible that a cow might actually be behind the chair in which I sat.

OBEMBE. She also pointed at me.

BEN (*as Mother*). *They're grazing everywhere Eme, why can't you see them?*

OBEMBE (*as Father*). *Will you shut up? What are you talking about? Good gracious – When did your children become cows grazing in our house?*

BEN (*as Mother*). *Leave me leave me, let me watch the shiny white cows.*

OBEMBE (*as Father*). *Shut up!*

BEN (*as Mother*). *Eme – leave me – leave me Eme – don't touch me – where are you taking me?*

(*Silence.*)

(*As himself.*) Mummy vanished for five weeks –

OBEMBE. Daddy had Mother committed –

BEN. I couldn't believe it – it felt like he betrayed her – he betrayed us – we didn't mind her grief –

OBEMBE. She scared me – I could tell she was never going to be the same –

BEN. They were cold and unnatural days –

OBEMBE. Did you know he kept her condition secret from people –

BEN. I once heard him tell our neighbours she had travelled to our village to stay with family and regain strength from the loss of our brothers –

OBEMBE. He always warned us –

BEN. Usually pulling at his right earlobe not to mention Mummy's illness to anyone –

OBEMBE (*as Father*). *Even the mosquito singing its seduction beside your ear must not hear it –*

BEN. After Mummy returned from the psychiatric hospital you found it –

OBEMBE. On the top shelf of the sitting-room display cabinet –

BEN. The framed portrait of Mummy and Daddy on their wedding day in 1979 –

OBEMBE. Next to it –

BEN. A small polythene bag containing grey and fluffy ash –

OBEMBE. It was tagged – Boja Agwu 1982–1996 – it was a sacrilege to Ani – Goddess of the Earth, for a person who committed suicide or fratricide to be buried in the earth –

BEN. At least we knew why we didn't know about Boja's funeral –

OBEMBE. Because there wasn't one –

(*Silence.*)

15.

OBEMBE. The list of his evils are endless – It was he, who took away our brothers –

BEN. It was he, who took away Father's job.

OBEMBE. It was he, who caused you and me to miss a school term.

BEN. It was he, who almost drove Mummy insane.

OBEMBE. It was he, who caused all of our brothers' possessions to be burned.

BEN. It was he, who caused Boja to be bloated like a balloon.

OBEMBE. It was he, who caused Ikenna to be obliterated by landfill.

BEN. It was he, who caused Boja's body to be burned like trash.

OBEMBE. It was he, who caused Boja to float around the town as a 'missing person'.

BEN. While his life has gone unscathed and untouched.

OBEMBE. He destroyed Daddy's map of dreams.

BEN. He birthed the spiders and cobwebs that invaded our house.

OBEMBE. It was he not Boja who planted the knife in Ikenna's body.

BEN. Obembe –

OBEMBE. What?

BEN. [I want to do it] – How do we kill Abulu?

(*Silence.*)

OBEMBE. We must conquer him here – In our minds and on our paper before we can conquer him in the flesh –

BEN. Pastor Collins has often said – (*As Pastor Collins*.) *whatever happens in the flesh, has already happened in the spiritual* –

OBEMBE. So before we leave in search of Abulu – We must first kill him here –

BEN. So what's the plan –

OBEMBE (*produces a piece of paper*). Here are my plans –

BEN. You are not serious – you have matchstick men on paper –

OBEMBE. This is not art class – It is not about my drawings – It's about the execution –

BEN. Okay – Okay – what's your idea?

OBEMBE. The first is the David-and-Goliath plan – We stone him to death –

BEN. With what boulders? – How many boulders can you lift not to mention throw? –

OBEMBE. A hunter's sling like David – A stone to Abulu's temple –

BEN. But how do we stone him? – Where? – And what time of day can we do it without being caught?

OBEMBE. We won't get caught –

BEN. And what if we stone him and hit someone else in the process? –

OBEMBE. You are right – Plan A is void (*Crosses out plan*)

BEN. What's Plan B?

OBEMBE. Look at it – (*Hands the sketch to* BEN.)

BEN. …This came out of your mind –

OBEMBE. The Okonkwo plan – After the story of *Things Fall Apart* –

BEN. This is very… scary –

OBEMBE. Haba – It's just a sketch –

BEN. Yes – the real thing will be worse –

OBEMBE. So it's a good plan –

BEN. What if he fights or stabs you first? –

OBEMBE. I would not want that –

BEN. Me neither – I think you should cross it out –

OBEMBE. Oh boy – I only had two – I thought they were good enough – We must come up with a plan together –

(*Silence*.)

What if we chased him and as he runs from us he wanders into the path of a moving car and spills the content of his head onto the road –

BEN. That plan will surely backfire –

OBEMBE. We will probably be the ones running away from him –

BEN. Into the path of a merciless vehicle –

OBEMBE. Not what we want –

(*Pause*.)

BEN. It felt like we thought of plans for days –

OBEMBE. We did –

BEN. Eventually, we decided to find and study the madman – We went in late mornings between ten and two in the afternoon –

OBEMBE. When Mummy and Daddy were at work –

BEN. We avoided the school routes to avoid our school friends –

OBEMBE. we searched the district for any sign of the madman – but found none –

BEN. You were not deterred Obembe and found Nonso at the petrol garage –

OBEMBE. Nonso had all the information –

BEN (*as Nonso*). *Small boys, what are you doing here?*
Shouldn't you be at school?

OBEMBE. We are in mourning for at least a term –

BEN (*as Nonso*). *Ah yes – I heard about what happened – Ike*
stabbed in the belly by his younger dude – I didn't know Boja
was wild sha – anyway, may their souls rest in peace –

OBEMBE. Are you minding these newspapers and magazines?

BEN (*as Nonso*). *Haven't you heard of me? – I am the only*
distributor in this district – This is my business –

OBEMBE. Oh – congratulations

BEN (*as Nonso*). *It's just the beginning –*

OBEMBE. My brother Ben and I want to know if you can help
us –

BEN (*as Nonso*). *Name it and I'll see what I can do –*

OBEMBE. Have you seen the madman Abulu? –

BEN (*as Nonso*). *That demon! – I saw him two days ago on this*
very same expressway [*leading to Benin*].

OBEMBE. Where? – Can you tell us?

BEN (*as Nonso*). *There was a mob on the side of the road down*
there next to the filling station – So I go and investigate – I
fight my way through the mob and I saw the dead body of a
woman – A victim of a hit-and-run – the blood in her hair
was still fresh and glistening on the road – then I saw that
demon on top of her – thrusting into her as everybody
watched – defiling the dead… he relieved himself and clung
on to the woman and fell asleep –

(*Silence.*)

16.

OBEMBE. At breakfast Mummy introduced Mr Bayo –

BEN (*as Mother*). *My princes, your daddy's friend Mr Bayo,
who moved to Canada has arrived and promised to take the
both of you to Canada with him. Allelujah – I have a God
who never fails – I have a God who never fails – Who never
fails – forever more.*

(*Mother carries on singing.*)

OBEMBE. What about our school?

BEN (*as Mother*). *Obembe, you will get a better school in
Canada –*

OBEMBE. Mummy, how will we adjust?

BEN (*as Mother*). *Just fine – Canada is one of the newest
countries in the world – The country has really developed
over a short period of time and even surpassed Britain – It
will be brilliant for you to be a part of that development –*

*It will soon become one of the most influential countries in
the world – Far from the ugly legacy of Gowan – better that
this useless and corrupt Nigeria —*

17.

OBEMBE. If it is true that we're going to Canada – then we
have to kill that madman as soon as possible – we have to
find him quickly –

BEN. Let's forget the madman and let's go and start a new life
in Canada.

OBEMBE. You're not serious – We have to kill him soon!

BEN.... Yes, Yes – We must...

(*Silence*.)

The day after Daddy announced our potential immigration to Canada –

OBEMBE *shoves a piece of paper into* BEN*'s hands*.

OBEMBE. We could kill him with otapiapia – We could buy one and put it in bread and give it to the madman, since he eats anything from anywhere –

BEN. That's true – but have you thought of why those years of feeding from these streets haven't killed him?

OBEMBE. The people of Akure town might think he is a supernatural being, who cannot be physically killed, but I don't believe any of that – he is still – just – a mortal man –

BEN. Are you sure?

OBEMBE. if we feed him poison bread, people will think he died from something he ate by himself from some garbage dump –

BEN. It was a very reasonable argument –

OBEMBE. We first went to the abandoned truck he frequently lived –

BEN. But he was not there –

OBEMBE. Yes he was – he was cooking –

BEN. That was after we went back – he was cooking?

OBEMBE. We saw him – pouring things – He stank –

BEN. He reeked of sweat – he stunk of [accumulated] sweat around his private parts and armpits –

OBEMBE. He smelt of rotten food –

BEN. Unhealed wounds and pus –

OBEMBE. Of urine and dry faeces –

BEN. Of old clothes and dead leaves –

OBEMBE. He smelled of the Omi-Ala water –

BEN. He smelled like a large rubbish bin –

OBEMBE. He smelled of rotten meat from the abattoir –

BEN. Of sewage water and filth –

OBEMBE. Of used condoms from the La Room Hotel –

BEN. Of semen,

OBEMBE. Of vaginal fluids

BEN. Of dried mucus –

    (*Silence*.)

OBEMBE (*approaching Abulu*)....We have some bread to spare – You want some? – You can have all of it

BEN (*as Abulu*). *Food – eat – rice – beans – eat bread eat – that – Amala – maize – eba – Yam – egg – eat – food – food – ajankroba – food – eat this – food – eat – eat*

OBEMBE. This is good food – Take it – Eat it – Eat Abulu /... [Mission accomplished – Let's not go too far away from him]

BEN (*panting*). Yes okay –

OBEMBE. He will soon fall –

BEN. I pitied him –

OBEMBE. I knew it –

BEN. What do you mean? You knew nothing –

OBEMBE. You looked tearful –

BEN. I did not –

OBEMBE. You did – how could you?

BEN. I pitied him

OBEMBE. You pitied him? – Why!?

BEN. Because he had nobody – he would die alone – that was it –

OBEMBE. why would that make you tearful? –

BEN. He reminded me of the pigeons

OBEMBE. Pigeons ke? –

BEN. Like the nursery rhymes we used to sing

OBEMBE. I don't remember any pigeons –

BOTH. Look at the pigeons – they have no clothes – they have no garden – and yet God watches them

OBEMBE. What has that got to do with anything?

BEN. I pitied the madman, because he reminded me of the pigeons –

OBEMBE. He ate the poisoned bread – he is dying – we avenged Ike and Boja – do you know how happy I am – now we will have peace – they will have peace – it's over… [do you know how many people we've helped – ourselves yes – but many – everyone ever afflicted by the menace of that interfering madman] – that demon is no longer amongst us –

(BEN *is horrified and startled as Abulu walks towards he and* OBEMBE.)

What is it – what are you looking at?

BEN. Abulu

OBEMBE. What? – Where? – How?… (*Sees Abulu.*) Wowuu!

BEN. He's dancing –

OBEMBE. And clapping –

BEN. It's a miracle –

OBEMBE. He's singing –

BEN. He just isn't dying – He is not of this world –

OBEMBE. Lie! He is a human being. I swear I will avenge my brothers. I will do it – The knife plan!

BEN. The knife plan?

OBEMBE. We will stab him and run away.

(*Silence*.)

We will do it tomorrow.

18.

BEN. Shortly after we got home – Daddy went out and did not return for the rest of the day

OBEMBE. It was a little after midnight – Daddy had still not returned

BEN. Mummy anxiously knocked on our neighbours' doors to raise the alarm –

OBEMBE. She did not know the whereabouts of her husband –

BEN. Our neighbours were sympathetic and reassured Mummy –

OBEMBE. Reassuring Mummy, Daddy would eventually return –

BEN. Daddy did return –

OBEMBE. I was asleep –

BEN. Mummy asked Daddy to give an account of himself –

OBEMBE. Daddy did not talk –

BEN. You asked him in the morning –

OBEMBE. For some reason –

BEN. He told you

OBEMBE (*as Father*). *I had a cataract operation – It's fine – it's fixed – no more questions –*

BEN. Daddy was changed – because even after his bandage was removed –

BEN. One of Daddy's eyelids could no longer close properly –

OBEMBE. Daddy was obsessed with when Nigeria would get better –

BEN. Daddy – when will we go to Canada –

OBEMBE (*as Father*). *Early next year* –

BEN. Early next year? –

OBEMBE (*as Father*). *Early next year?* –

BEN. It must be January –

OBEMBE (*as Father*). *Yes, you're right January,*

19.

(OBEMBE *lights a cigarette*.)

BEN. You're still smoking – You will remain the height of a ten-year-old forever

OBEMBE. You want some?

BEN. Please not near me…

OBEMBE.…

BEN. you know I can still smell it…

(*A faint Christmas carol can be heard.*)

OBEMBE.…It shall be this night –

BEN. That's a Christmas carol –

OBEMBE. The consumers' holiday…

BEN. Predominantly food – all the Christmas recipes –

OBEMBE. Live-roasters –

BEN. Guinea fowl –

OBEMBE. Rice –

BEN. Tomatoes –

OBEMBE. Spinach

BEN. Shrimp –

OBEMBE. Pounded yam

BOTH. Supermalt… (*After consideration*.) palm wine –

(*Silence*.)

OBEMBE. this night – I have the knife ready – once we are sure Daddy and Mummy are asleep, we will leave through the window – will I be going alone?

BEN (*stammering*)….No I'll come with you –

(*Silence*.)

OBEMBE. But you didn't –

BEN. You know what happened –

OBEMBE. it was planned – you fell asleep in the living room with Daddy and I came to wake you –

BEN. You didn't come to wake me –

OBEMBE. I shook you from behind the single sofa –

BEN. I didn't feel anything – I was fast asleep –

OBEMBE. You pretended to snore –

BEN. I did not pretend – I snore – when I sleep I snore –

OBEMBE. I shook you – you pretended to snore – it nearly woke Daddy – I took cover behind the sofa – I waited until the coast was clear and went by myself –

BEN. what you wanted –

OBEMBE. It's what *you* wanted –

BEN. I slow you down anyway – you said that before –

OBEMBE. You were still supposed to come with me –

BEN. Well, I was fast asleep –

OBEMBE. That's what you say –

BEN. But you didn't catch him anyway –

OBEMBE. The idiot wasn't there – otherwise I would have killed him –

(*Silence.*)

I went out a few times –

BEN. A few times?

OBEMBE. In that week – I would get to the abandoned truck and the madman wouldn't be there –

BEN. On Christmas Day you stared out of the window while Father talked about the money he's sent to Mr Bayo for our journey –

OBEMBE. You stayed with me on New Year's Eve while the fireworks lit up the dark outside –

BEN. I couldn't read your mind – I wanted you to tell me something – to talk to me –

(*Silence.*)

20.

OBEMBE (*as Father*). *I am leaving for Lagos right now – I'm taking your photographs with me to apply for your travel passports – Bayo will have arrived in Nigeria by the time I return and then we will go together to Lagos for your Canadian visa – I'm leaving you two fifty-naira notes... be careful –*

BEN. After breakfast

OBEMBE. We went to fetch water –

BEN. You announced –

OBEMBE. The final attempt – we will go find him once
    Mummy is asleep –

BEN. Do we have to?

OBEMBE. Yes! – The river – we will go with our hooked
    fishing rods –

(*Silence*.

BEN *nods*.)

I have traced him two times now to the river – he seems to
go there every evening –

he goes there to bathe – then he sits under the mango tree
where we first saw him – if we kill him there – no one will
find out –

BEN. the fishing rods?

OBEMBE. they are now long barbed sticks with sickle-like
    hooks attached to their ends – they are perfect –

BEN. you've adapted them –

OBEMBE. they're under the bed – in our bedroom –

BEN. What about Father? – our school with white people? –

OBEMBE. We have to get this done –

BEN. No Obe – let's not do it – Look we're going to Canada –
    we're going to live there, let us not do it – Let us go – we
    grow up and become like Chuck Norris or Commando and
    come here and shoot him with big guns –

OBEMBE. You are fool – you don't know what you are saying
    – you want us to run away to Canada? Where is Ikenna?
    Where is Boja? You don't know – but I know, I know where
    they are – I don't need your help – I will do it by myself –

BEN. No, no Obe – I will go with you –

OBEMBE. YOU WON'T –

(BEN *gets on his knees*.)

BEN. Please don't do it without me – I still want to do it for our brothers too –

OBEMBE. don't you want to go Canada any more?

BEN. Not without you –

(OBEMBE *paces then stops*.

Silence.)

OBEMBE. Stand up –

(BEN *gets off his knees*.)

Listen, I want to go to Canada, too – that's exactly why I want us to do this quickly and pack our things – You know that Father has gone to get the visas?

(BEN *nods*.)

Listen we will be unhappy if we leave Nigeria without doing it – let me tell you – I am older than you and I know much more than you do –

(BEN *nods*.)

So I am telling you, now listen, if we go to Canada without doing this, we will hate it there – We will not be happy – Do you want to be unhappy?

BEN. No

OBEMBE. Me neither –

BEN. Let us go – I want to do it.

OBEMBE. Is that the truth?

BEN. The truth

OBEMBE. The truth?

BEN (*nodding*). Yes the truth.

OBEMBE. Okay, let us go then –

(OBEMBE *grabs two torches and gives one to* BEN.)

In case we have to wait till it gets pitch dark – We're about to avenge our brothers Ikenna and Boja. Ben, take up your fishing rod –

(OBEMBE *grabs the bag*.)

OBEMBE. *We trail behind our lines*.

BEN. *We trail behind our lines*.

OBEMBE. *Hook, line and sinkers*.

BEN. *Hook, line and sinkers*.

OBEMBE. *We are Fishermen*.

BEN. *We are Fishermen*.

BOTH. *Fishermen*

21.

OBEMBE. We will avoid places where we might be seen by people who already know our story – who would gaze at us with sympathy

BEN. Or suspicion

OBEMBE. By the Esan, stinging bushes by the path to the river is where we will wait for the madman –

(*Abulu singing and clapping*.)

Shhh –

BEN. He is there, let us attack him now –

OBEMBE. No – we have to wait a bit, to make sure no one is coming, then we will go and kill him –

BEN. But it is getting too dark –

OBEMBE. Don't worry – that helps – let's make sure no one is around for when we do it –

BEN. Your voice cracked –

OBEMBE. clean your ears jor –

BEN. We can still –

OBEMBE. What?

BEN. ...Be like those ferocious matchstick men you drew –

OBEMBE. Take your fishing rod

BEN (*whispering*). okay...

(*Silence.*)

OBEMBE. Ready?

BEN. okay...

OBEMBE. Ben are you afraid –   .

BEN. Yes I am –

OBEMBE. Listen – do not be afraid – we are doing the right thing and God knows, we will be free.

(OBEMBE *embraces* BEN.)

BEN. Let's do it quickly –

OBEMBE. Abulu was lying on his back – facing the sky – Ready?... Go! –

BEN. We ran out of our hiding place towards the river –

OBEMBE. The madman's eyes were closed –

BEN (*with a frantic cry*). Attack –

OBEMBE. jab the hook lines at his chest – his face – his hand – his head – his neck

BEN *crying and weeping.*

with the hooks – slice into his flesh – bore bleeding holes – and rip out chucks of his flesh

BEN. pieces of flesh dropping from his body and blood everywhere streaming down, dripping off his torso –

OBEMBE. Abulu did not expect it –

BEN. We attacked him with all our anger –

OBEMBE. We kept hitting – pulling hooks and flesh –

BEN. Abulu stumbled about –

OBEMBE. We kept hitting –

BEN. Pulling –

OBEMBE. Striking –

BEN. Screaming –

OBEMBE. Crying

BEN. Sobbing –

OBEMBE. Covered in blood

BEN. Abulu fell into the water –

OBEMBE. With a large wild splash?

BEN. You ran off. Where did you go?

OBEMBE. I saw the silhouette of two men running toward us – torches flashing

BEN. Before I could move – one of them was there – holding my shorts from behind – the smell of alcohol was heavy on him – he wrestled me to the ground – calling to his friend in an unfamiliar...

OBEMBE. I was calling you as I ran away – the other one was gaining on me –

BEN. The man held my left arm in a tight grip – in the struggle to wrestle myself free – I grabbed the fishing rod and hit the man with the hook end with all my strength – he cried out – his torch fell down and lit up his soldier's boots –

OBEMBE. One of the soldiers assigned to patrol Omi-Ala –

BEN. I ran away as far as I could between houses and bush paths and when I reached Abulu's decrepit truck – I stopped and dropped to my knees – gasping for life – for air – As I stooped on the ground, I saw the soldier that chased you now running back to the river – I ducked behind Abulu's truck making sure he had not seen me – I waited – still

(*Silence.*

OBEMBE *runs on and retches.*)

OBEMBE (*whispering*). Ben –

BEN. Obe –

OBEMBE. Where's your fishing rod?

BEN. I left it there –

OBEMBE. why

BEN. It stuck in the man's hand –

OBEMBE. how did that happen? –

BEN (*nods*). He almost caught me – so I hit him with it –

OBEMBE. Okay – we will hide my own fishing line at the back of Mummy's tomato garden – Take off your shirt and throw it over the back fence –

BEN. [I retched.]

OBEMBE. Don't worry – it is finished –

BEN. . . . [It is finished –]

(OBEMBE *embraces* BEN.

Silence.)

22.

BEN (*as Mother*). *Pastor Collins has been here since six waiting for you? – Where are your shirts?*

OBEMBE. The heat Mummy – we were soaked in sweat –

BEN (*as Mother*). *And – look at you Benjamin – Your head is all covered in mud – tell me where did you go?*

OBEMBE. We've been playing football on a pitch by the public high school – we will go and get cleaned up –

BEN (*as Mother*). *Stand where you are, Pastor Collins wants to pray for you before he leaves –*

(BEN *and* OBEMBE *remain in the room as Pastor Collins hovers his palm above their heads to pray for the children.*)

OBEMBE (*as Pastor Collins*). *I ask oh heavenly father that you help these children move on after the tragic events of last year – help them to succeed in their quest to travel oversees – and bless them both – make the officials at the Canadian embassy grant them the visas – Oh God – For thou art able to make all things right – thou art able – You know oh God – How this woman has suffered – so much – so much for the kids – you know all things oh Lord – wipe her tears – wipe her tears Jesus – let her not have any cause to cry over her children again – Amen*

BEN (*as Mother*). *Go right away into the bathroom and clean up…*

(*Silence.*

BEN *and* OBEMBE *kneel at a plastic bucket cleaning themselves up.*)

OBEMBE (*elated*). Ben – we did it – we avenged them – Ike and Boja

(OBEMBE *embraces* BEN.)

Do you know what it means? Esan – reckoning – I know that without it our brothers would never forgive us and we could never be free – this water is a little too cold – your turn – be quick –

(BEN *nodding*

BEN*'s hands are shaking and drops the cup he's using to scoop water.*)

BEN. My hands are shaky – really shaking.

OBEMBE. I told you to be quick –

BEN. I was trying to focus on the insect train from the thin crack in the wall –

OBEMBE. that didn't help – it made you dizzy – ahh Ben, Ben – look me in the eyes – Are you afraid?

(BEN *nods.*)

Why? Why? – Ati gba esun – we have achieved reckoning – why? Why? Why? Fisherman Ben are you afraid?

BEN....those soldiers – I'm afraid of them – I'm afraid they will – I'm afraid the soldiers will come for us and kill us – all of us –

OBEMBE. lower your volume – the soldiers won't – they won't – they don't know us – don't even think like that – they don't know where we are or who we are – they didn't see you come here did they?

(BEN *shakes his head.*)

OBEMBE. So why then do you fear – there's nothing to be afraid of – listen – days will decay – like food – this night will decay too – and you will forget – we will forget – nothing will happen to us – nothing – no one will touch us – Father will come back tomorrow and take us to Mr Bayo's and we will go to Canada... you see it

BEN (*nods*)....what about Daddy and Mummy? – Will the soldiers not touch them either –

OBEMBE. No they won't – (*Punching fist in palm.*) they will be fine – happy and will always come to Canada to see us

BEN. Tell me – what about you Obe?

OBEMBE. Me? Me? –

BEN. Be'ni – Yes, I said – I said –

OBEMBE. I. will. be. fine. – You. will. be. fine. – Daddy will be fine – Mummy will be fine ehn – all – everything will be fine –

(BEN *nods.*

Silence.)

23.

BEN. We were eating our beans when Mother returned singing and dancing –

OBEMBE. Mummy, what is it?

BEN (*as Mother*). *My God has finally vanquished my enemy – Chineke na 'eme nma, ime le eke le diri gi –*

Abulu, Onye Ojo a wungo – Abulu, the evil one is dead – they said he was killed near Omi-Ala – You see it was my God that kept you safe when you were going to that place to fish – Imagine the body of that evil man lying there? You see, my chi is alive and has finally avenged me – Abulu lashed my children with his tongue and now that tongue will rot in his mouth forever –

(*Pause.*)

OBEMBE. Mummy was so happy –

BEN. When we returned to our room to sleep – you didn't say anything – we went to sleep and I saw you –

OBEMBE. you saw me? – I was sleeping

BEN. I woke up and you were talking –

OBEMBE. Talking? To who? – how?

BEN. Yourself –

OBEMBE. You're making it up –

BEN. You said – (*As Obembe, dream-like.*) *I did it for you, we, Ben and I, we did it for you – both of you, – I'm sorry for this Mummy and Daddy – I'm sorry, we did it so you may not suffer any more…*

OBEMBE. And? –

BEN. You just started sobbing –

OBEMBE. I don't remember that –

(*Silence.*)

BEN. It was the first time I noticed you had lost so much weight

OBEMBE. I've put that back on now –

BEN. You need to give some away –

OBEMBE. never – it's a sign of wealth –

BEN. You don't look wealthy –

OBEMBE. It's a figure of speech – haven't you heard?

(*Silence.*)

24.

(*Commotion out in the street.*)

OBEMBE. Mama – what is the noise about?

BEN (*as Mother*). *Abulu – they are taking his body away in a truck and they say that soldiers are going about searching for the ones that killed him – I don't understand these people really – why can't someone kill that useless person? Why should they not kill him? What if he's put fear in their mind that some evil will befall them? Who should blame them?*

OBEMBE. You said – (*As Ben.*) *Do the soldiers want to kill them?*

BEN (*as Mother*). *No I don't know if they will kill them – Anyway both of you should stay indoors – no going out until this has cooled down – You will lock the gate after me as I go to the shop – be sure to open the gate for Eme when he returns – he will come in the afternoon*

OBEMBE. Why did you say that in Mummy's presence ehn? Are you stupid? Do you want her to fall sick again? Do you want to destroy us again?

BEN. No – I just wanted to know about the soldiers –

OBEMBE. Listen – they must not find out you hear? –

(BEN *nodding.*)

…Don't worry, we will lock the door and go into Ikenna and Boja's and sit on the new new mattress until Daddy returns –

BEN. What if they climb the fence and come in or if they –

OBEMBE. Let's wait here –

(*Silence.*)

BEN. We must have remained motionless on the floor for hours –

OBEMBE (*as Father*). *Obembe? Ben? – Are you alright both of you – What are you doing in here?*

BEN. Yes Daddy! – We remembered Ike and Boja

OBEMBE (*as Father*). *Oh good gracious – Listen, I want both of you to put all that behind you from now on – look at your mother – look at what happened to her – that woman has suffered a lot – why, because of the love she has for her children. The love I mean for you – all of you – now, I'm telling you – both of you henceforth, before you do anything, anything at all, think first of her, of what it might do to her – only and only then should you make your decision. I'm not even asking you to think of me – think of her. Do you hear me? – And you know what is more? Bayo is now in Nigeria. I called Atinuke yesterday and spoke with him, he will be here to take you to Lagos for your visas next week.*

BEN. Next week?

(*Silence.*)

25.

OBEMBE. Ben wake up, wake up Ben – Come, stand up, we have to leave this night –

BEN. What leave home? –

OBEMBE. Yes right now – Listen the soldiers can find us – I saw Mama Iyabo while I was running away from the soldier and she recognised me – I almost knocked her down –

BEN. Why didn't you tell me before?

OBEMBE. I have been afraid that she would tell them it was us – so, let us leave now – they could still come this night – and they too might identify us. I have been awake and I've heard voices outside all night – if they don't, they will surely come in the morning or any time –

BEN. So, what should we do?

OBEMBE. We must leave, that's the only way – it is the only way we can protect ourselves and our parents – Mummy especially –

BEN. Where would we go?

OBEMBE. Anywhere – (*Starts to cry.*) let's just go –

BEN. Obe – but –

OBEMBE. Won't you move from there now?

BEN. No, where shall we go?

OBEMBE. They will search here in the morning – And they will find us – they'll find us / they will find us

BEN. But I'm afraid Obe – we should not have killed him –

OBEMBE. Don't say this – he killed our brothers – he deserved to die –

BEN. Daddy will get us a good lawyer – we shouldn't leave Obe…

OBEMBE. listen, don't be stupid – the soldiers will kill us – we wounded their man, they will shoot us –

Imagine, what will happen to Mummy – Nigeria is a military government – Abacha's soldiers are no-nonsense – let's go somewhere – Mummy and Daddy can then arrange to meet us, take us to Ibadan and then Canada –

BEN….Okay –

OBEMBE. then pack, quick, quick, quick, quick I can hear Mummy's voice – she is praying – she might come in here to see us –

(*They leave.*)

26.

(*Running away.*

A while later BEN *stops*.)

OBEMBE. What happened? Why have you stopped? –

BEN. I want to go back –

OBEMBE. What? Benjamin, are you mad?

BEN. I want to go back –

OBEMBE. Come on –

BEN. No, no, don't come – don't come –

   (OBEMBE *starts to walk towards* BEN.)

   …just let me go back –

OBEMBE. Wait – wait – I won't touch you –

   (OBEMBE *walks over to* BEN *and embraces him.*
   OBEMBE *tries to push* BEN *forwards. They struggle.*

   They stop from breathlessness.)

   Ben!… If you won't come with me – then tell them – tell
   Daddy and Mummy that I ran… I ran away – tell them that
   we – me – I made you do it –

   (OBEMBE *leaves*.)

BEN….Will you write to me?

   (OBEMBE *does not respond*.)

   I don't want you to go – Obembe! Come back! I can't do it
   on my own – I'm afraid Obembe –

   Please come back –

   (BEN *cries painfully*

   Silence.)

27.

BEN. After you ran – but even before, after our brothers died –
I was no longer myself – I had never lived without my
brothers – without knowing your leadership –

Codes and rules to get through life – I had never really ever
done anything without you – knowing where I was going –
you were my oracle – the one who had learned from our
eldest two – a true professor of information – I would always
think anything I had to say through without – thinking it
must be profound for you to actually acknowledge me –
When Ikenna and Boja died, you prevented me from the
sense of loss – where I might have broken down – by always
talking to me – I had to now stand at every door shaking
with dread – knowing really I wasn't quite ready – I got back
home and our room was empty and dark – and all I could do
was just lay there on the floor crying – thinking of you
running – your rucksack on your back – a raffia Ghana-
Must-Go bag in your hand – dragging your feet – panting
and sweating – running as far as your feet could carry you
like Clemens Forell –

OBEMBE. Clemens Forell?

BEN. Yes the same –

OBEMBE. The luckiest German to escape a Soviet Gulag –
I can't say I had that presence of thought… I was just
running –

BEN. I just thought you probably ran to the very end of the
longest road. You must have got tired. You must have
become thirsty. Did you just run on with fear or did you
think about me? Were you thinking about me? – I woke up
the next morning to the sound of gunshots in the air and
people shouting – hands banging on doors – people rushing
around – six soldiers were banging at our gate – once Father
opened they shoved him out of the way.

(*As Soldier.*) *Where are they? Where are those juvenile delinquents – murderers?* (*As himself.*) They stamped their boots through our house – in our hall I could hear Mummy falling to her knees.

(*As Mother.*) *Please, please officers – they are innocent – they are innocent.*

(*As himself.*) The soldier told Mummy – (*As Soldier.*) *Shut up – where are those boys? I want them delivered to me right now*

(*As himself.*) Our door to our bedroom was being booted.

(*As Soldier.*) *You boys will open now or I will blast your heads.*

(*As himself.*) So I unlatched the door and I was arrested. Because of my age – the judge deemed me unworthy of a life imprisonment, or capital punishment and not worthy of juvenile prison because I had committed murder.

(*As Judge.*) *You will be held till society deems you an adult, able to conduct yourself in a civilised way acceptable to the society and mankind. In light of this, and by the powers conferred in me by the Federal Justice System of the Federal Republic of Nigeria, and by the recommendation of the jury that justice be tempered with mercy – for the sake of your parents, Mr and Mrs Agwu, I hearby sentence you Benjamin Azikiwe Agwu, to eight years' confinement without familial contacts – until, you shall reach the societal-proved maturity age of eighteen. The court is hereby dismissed.*

(*As himself.*) The prison policy allowed a preacher to visit inmates. An Evangelist came every fortnight and he was the one that told me I'll be released in the spirit of the first ever transition of military-to-civilian rule in Nigeria – Olusegun Agagu had decided to free some prisoners – Father told me my name had topped the list.

28.

OBEMBE. So here you are –

BEN. here I am… and so are you

OBEMBE. I had to wait for you – When I ran – I took a bus
from Akure to Benin City – I saw a woman getting out of a
car and I told her I had nowhere to sleep and she took pity on
me – six months of being adopted by her – I got homesick so
I came back –

BEN. You came back?

OBEMBE. Once! I got back here and I was too scared to enter
our compound – so I told our neighbour Igbafe – I told him I
would write to you and for him to deliver the letter – all I
could think about was you –

BEN. really? –

OBEMBE. All the time – I'm surprised I wasn't suspected of
taking a new lover

BEN. You're a lover now? –

OBEMBE. I have done many things whilst… since we have
been apart –

BEN. Lucky you –

OBEMBE. I wasn't happy –

BEN. I'll take your word for it… It's good to see you –

(*Beat.*)

Mummy and Daddy will probably be wondering where I am
– I have to go –

OBEMBE. Do you still? – can you still face it – Mummy and
Daddy?

BEN. why do you want to take on full blame? –

OBEMBE. It stayed with me... what I heard – I should have kept it to myself – but I told Ikenna he would be killed by a fisherman – He asked and I really thought I was being helpful – I was so stupid – so stupid – listen Ben – even you have suffered because of me –

BEN. Yes!... but you weren't to know –

OBEMBE. I will live with it – I have been living with it

BEN. We are all living with it... I too conjured the curse – the prophecy into motion –

OBEMBE. Your portion is that you followed your elder brothers dutifully –

BEN. But I also instigated – It was me that said we should behead Mama Iyabo's hen – and you need blood sacrifice from an animal for a prophecy to come true –

OBEMBE....I want to go to them – our parents – but I can't face them alone –

BEN....

OBEMBE. You are released now and I said... I'm here, I said I would –

BEN. Need me –

OBEMBE. Can we meet them together? To, to beg for forgiveness for all we've done – for what they a have suffered – Ben, please – will you do this with me... it's me Obe – your brother – do you hear me?

BEN. I do.

OBEMBE. Will you take me home with you?

(BEN *begins to sing*.)

BEN....Iyoghogho Iyogho Iyoghogho, ka'nyi je na nke Bishopu na five akwola, ihe ne ewe m'iwe bun a efe'm akorako, Nwa'm bun a-afo na'ewe ahuli... Sing with me –

BOTH (*singing*). ka'nyi je na nke Bishopu na five akwola, ihe
ne ewe m'iwe bun a efe'm akorako, Nwa'm bun a-afo
na'ewe ahuli

[Let us go to the Bishop's it is five o'clock, I'm only sad
because my laundry is still wet, but I'm relieved to know that
the child in my womb is happy.]

(*The brothers leave together.*

The End.)

A Nick Hern Book

This stage adaptation of *The Fishermen* first published in Great Britain in 2018 as a paperback original by Nick Hern Books Limited, The Glasshouse, 49a Goldhawk Road, London W12 8QP, in association with New Perspectives and HOME

The Fishermen copyright © 2015 Chigozie Obioma
First published in Great Britain by Little, Brown and Company in 2015

This stage adaptation of *The Fishermen* copyright © 2018 Gbolahan Obisesan
Gbolahan Obisesan has asserted his right to be identified as the author of this adaptation

Designed and typeset by Nick Hern Books, London
Printed in Great Britain by Mimeo Ltd, Huntingdon, Cambridgeshire PE29 6XX

A CIP catalogue record for this book is available from the British Library

ISBN 978 1 84842 797 6

www.nickhernbooks.co.uk

facebook.com/nickhernbooks

twitter.com/nickhernbooks